Inspired, No

Inspired, Not Retired

INSPIRED, NOT RETIRED

Inspired, Not Retired

Inspired, Not Retired

"Real Leaders grasp that excellence in the Leadership craft doesn't just come from experience. It comes when you dedicate the time to reflect on and learn from that experience. If you want an aid to reflect and learn about leadership; buy this book, read this book and use this book. Your team, your peers and your boss will thank you."

Vincent E. Boles
Major General (MG), US Army, Retired
Founder, *Vincent E. Boles, LLC*
Author of **4-3-2-1 Leadership***: What America's Sons and Daughters Taught Me on My Way from Second Lieutenant to Two-Star General*

"With this book, Dr. Randolph challenges leaders to think deeper, driving better decisions on how to be a more effective leader. By using storytelling and real-life experiences, he breaks down the process allowing for easier execution. A must read!"

Michael J. Parejko
Chief Executive Officer
Mississippi Valley Regional Blood Center

"I grew up in a single parent home raised by my mother. I sometimes envied Burl for having that extra parental resource. I do believe that by being friends with Burl throughout high school I picked up some secondary effects of his father that flowed from Burl, Sr., to Burl, Jr., on to me."

Lonnie Johnson
Chief Information Officer
KVC Health Systems, Inc

Inspired, Not Retired

INSPIRED, NOT RETIRED

Leadership Lessons from Father to Son

Dr. Burl Randolph, Jr., DM

Inspired, Not Retired

Inspired, Not Retired

My father, Burl W. Randolph, inspired this book. He taught me
that retirement does not mean the end of
working or living.

This book is dedicated to my sons, Dominic and Derek Randolph,

who taught me that being a father is my true inspiration.

Dominic (L) and Derek Randolph practicing
Taekwondo moves, 2006.

Derek (L), me, and Dominic Randolph at the White
House Press Podium, 2007.

Inspired, Not Retired

Contents

FOREWORD

I have had the privilege of knowing Dr. Burl Randolph Jr. since we were freshmen in high school. We met in Junior ROTC and immediately bonded around our passion for the ROTC lifestyle. I think we were both two introverts who enjoyed being isolated in the basement of the school. There we had great structure and we discovered a newfound happiness with the discovery of how precise things could be executed.

Everything about our lives was not always disciplined and structured. We were young boys for goodness sake, and we grew up in a pretty rough neighborhood. Our zip code, 64130, had the most crime of the entire Kansas City, Missouri metropolitan area. And it still does over 40 years later. But during that time, we found a great sense of stability at school and at home.

Mr. Randolph

My first encounter with Burl's father was when our other ROTC buddy, James Burton who is no longer with us, stopped by to pick Burl up to go hang out and do teenager stuff. When we walked in the house, Mr. Randolph was solemn but kind and inviting. He had the type of personality that commanded respect. He had an air about him that automatically made you want to stand up straight and be well mannered. He had a humble reverence about him. His smile was kind but reserved. He didn't allow you to get too familiar as this was how things were in those days.

You respected your elders, and Burl Randolph Sr. was a guy that you felt was due such honor and respect. We were always on our best behavior around him. He never spoke a harsh word to us nor threatened to speak with our parents about our behavior. Again, he had an air about him that just made you want to be on your best behavior.

The Burl I Know

Fast forward several years later to today and I can see a lot of his mannerisms in Dr. Burl Randolph, Jr. He carries that same air. One that commands respect. I had not been in touch with Burl in over 25 years after high school as we had gone our separate ways. On rare occasions we would touch bases electronically. I followed his career over that time and was always very proud of his many accomplishments.

Then one day Burl was in town, reached out to me, and asked if he could come visit me. I invited him to stop by my job. I had accomplished a few things I was also proud of. I am one of the top executives of a national organization that does child welfare; I started my own 501c3 nonprofit (Growth Ministries, Inc) that helps felons reenter society; and I serve on the board of the largest homeless shelter in the Midwest. But I was still a bit nervous about his arrival after all these years.

Looking back at that moment I think I was nervous because his life had been so disciplined and well executed. I honestly believe that was because of his upbringing and the great input he received daily from his father. I grew up in a single parent home raised by my mother. I sometimes envied Burl for having that extra parental resource. I do believe that by being friends with Burl throughout high school I picked up some secondary effects of his father that flowed from Burl, Sr., to Burl, Jr., on to me.

Lonnie Johnson
Chief Information Officer
KVC Health Systems, Inc

Lonnie Johnson was born in Kansas City, Missouri, and has been a career management information technology officer in the Kansas City area for over 40 years. His education is in computer science and he is certified in ITIL Foundations 3.0 and ICAgile Certified Professional. He rose through the ranks in KVC from Director of Management Information Systems to Vice President for Business Information Technology to his current position of Chief Information Officer. KVC Health Systems is a private, nonprofit 501(c)3 organization and a national leader in behavioral healthcare, child welfare, and community health and wellness. Lonnie also founded ProDev, a website and software development company for commercial and personal websites.

Lonnie and Burl first met in the Junior Reserve Officer Training Corps (JROTC) class at Paseo High School in 1977. After joining the drill teams, color guard, and rifle marksmanship team, they formed a drill team at the John Thornberry Boys and Girls Club. They participated in drill team competitions across Kansas City and throughout Missouri, leading their teams to First Place standings. Their love of helping others and respect for each other's accomplishments brought them back together after Burl retired.

Master Sergeant John H. Scott, US Army, Retired, served as the Senior Army Instructor (SAI) for the Paseo High School JROTC program. His mentorship allowed Lonnie, me, and many other cadets the sanctuary to learn about leadership and excel.

Spring 1979, Sophomore year. Having fun in JROTC in front of Paseo High School. From left to right: Cadet Captain Lonnie Johnson; Cadet First Lieutenant Burl Randolph, Jr.; Cadet Major Hugh Berkley.

AUTHOR'S NOTE

"Strong minds discuss ideas, average minds discuss events, weak minds discuss people." –Socrates

"A hard head makes a soft behind." –Burl Randolph

Dad was a man of few but insightful words. In my youth, I did not always understand, but over time I learned he was exhibiting the key quality of all great patriarchs: Leadership. Dad's sayings were precise, concise, and always fit the situation. I do not remember Dad talking about people in a derogatory manner. People change like the weather, he figured, so what's the use? What he said throughout the years always inspired me, kept me focused on what I must do, and allowed me to pursue what I wanted more than anything else: being a Soldier.

Sometime after retirement, Dad told me, "A man ought to always stay busy." With most of his friends already gone to the great beyond and his fishing buddy, me, off to college, staying busy must have been a chore for Dad. I did not know the true significance of his comment until many years later. When Dad became ill from his second round of cancer, he told me he was convinced that the inactivity from his retirement had caused his illness. I then realized what Dad meant about staying busy, and what inactivity could do to a person.

Dad inspired me to always stay busy and purposeful for nearly 32 years, and why I remain *Inspired, Not Retired* after retiring from the Army.

After much reflection, I categorized Dad's sayings as Leadership Lesson's from Father to Son. Documenting the lessons of men like my father is so important because of the assault on the fatherhood record of African American males. Rarely is a success story told about the relationship between African American males and their children, specifically with their sons. The world needs positive stories about familial relationships, hope, and the promise created by great parenting, regardless of race or ethnicity. I hope you find these leadership lessons helpful in whatever journey you take. These lessons were beneficial to me throughout my life, and I pray they will inspire you as well.

Dr. Burl

(L) BenElla Randolph (R) Burl Randolph pinning Second Lieutenant Burl Randolph, Jr., Kemper Military School and College, May 1983

Inspired, Not Retired

Inspired, Not Retired

CHAPTER ONE
RETIREMENT IS IN THE EYES OF THE BEHOLDER

It's my retirement and I'll cry if I want too.

Have you ever just wanted to do nothing? Just lay in bed all day under the sheets, shutting out the sunlight, cellphones, and the world? This was always my dream for retirement, a dream that has yet to come to fruition. But in 2014, married to a working spouse, raising two teenage sons, and completing the second year of my doctoral studies, I realized I was just not built to relax, nor was I ready for retirement.

My Dad lived about 15 years in retirement before he died, but I am uncertain how much of it he enjoyed. Minus the six- or seven-years battling cancer, what I remember most about Dad in retirement was the one piece of advice he shared with me and my brothers, albeit at separate times:

"A man ought to always stay busy"

I also remember Dad talking about all the things he could have done. His list of shoulda-coulda-woulda's were not meant to bring fame and fortune, but for him to stay engaged with life.

After Dad died, my life went into overdrive and never really slowed down until retirement. Although retired from the Army after serving nearly 32 years, I remain inspired to carry out my calling to *Help Leaders Design Legacies That Last* ©. Believe me, that keeps me busy!

Although I learned from my Dad throughout my life, the most profound lessons were during his retirement from 1976 to 1991. This time span covered my high school and college years and my first tour on Active Duty. The chapters ahead are aligned semi-chronologically by the years Dad provided the life lessons, some of which were prior to his retirement. They are divided into three parts: The Insight, The Inspiration, and The Application. There is also a Notes Page in some chapters, to provide space for the reader to record thoughts and reduce the white space.

I would be remiss if I did not begin a leadership book without writing about my own leadership background. As a Doctor of Management in Organizational Leadership (DM), I am expected to be the expert in both management and leadership. After retirement, I formed my own business leadership and management consulting company, MyWingman, LLC. The doctoral leadership journey helped me to encapsulate and explain all my leadership expertise and experiences from emerging leader through Chief Executive Officer (CEO) and business owner in manners civilians can understand. This includes the ability to provide business coaching at every leadership and management level; forming, leading, and facilitating peer advisory groups; and designing mentoring programs. Although I am also versed in all aspects of organizational planning and performance management, the focus of my degree and this book is leadership.

Most of my background was in military leadership and I saw my doctoral studies as a transition point into civilian life. I have led or managed at various levels since I was 14 years old. Those experiences occurred through either the Junior Reserve Officer Training Corps (JROTC), student government in high school, Senior ROTC (SROTC) in college, business ownership in college (Cover to Cover Comics), military organizations, business organizations and affiliations, and community service.

Because I have extensive management and leadership experience, part of the doctoral studies requirement was to either develop or adapt my own leadership philosophy. Of all the numerous leadership definitions, I adopted what Dr. John Kotter wrote, "Management is about coping with complexity. Leadership is about coping with change." [1] Dr. Kotter explained that management produces order and consistency through planning and budgeting, organizing and staffing, and controlling and problem solving. These tasks strive for efficiency and effectiveness, which in turn creates complexity. This is best demonstrated through an organization's day-to-day, week-to-week, and month-to-month operations.

Some may consider these functions routine, but there is nothing routine about management and leadership. In both of Kotter's definitions on management and leadership, there was a consistent underlying theme: coping. Managers and leaders must cope with executing change within their respective environments because neither management nor leadership is an exact science.

This book is not so much about the culmination of management functions, but the consideration of the leadership functions that help manage change. Throughout my years as both a manger and a leader, I found management decidedly easier once viewed through Kotter's lens. Leadership is about the one factor people resist most: change. Although leadership has any number of definitions just as pithy but profound as Kotter's, this book is about the leadership lessons from a father to his son.

The Father of Modern Management, Peter Drucker, wrote that leadership is best defined by the desired ends.[2] Bernard Bass wrote, "The meaning of leadership may depend on the kind of institution in which it is found".[3] I agree with all the scholarly definitions, but as a practitioner and military man, I was humbled when I read what Shelley Kirkpatrick and Edwin Locke wrote that ."…leaders are not like other people"[4] and by a descriptive and accurate leadership definition:

> "Leadership is a demanding, unrelenting job with enormous pressures and grave responsibilities. It would be a profound disservice to leaders to suggest that they are ordinary people who happened to be in the right place at the right time."[5]

If you have ever led any organization, and I mean truly led it for the good of the people, this description of leadership should resonate within your soul.

Leadership is demanding and unrelenting. Not everyone you lead will gravitate to your leadership style or vision. The enormous pressures of leading can add to the stresses and unrelenting pace of the job. Grave responsibilities are not confined to the battlefield. The business owner, President, and Chief Executive Officer (CEO) make decisions that impact people's livelihoods. Employees may be laid off or fired. Some businesses may even become extinct. A leader must right-size their organization based on the current operating environment. These are the types of decisions I believe Kirkpatrick and Locke not only wrote about but experienced when describing leadership.

I envy those who have the rosy and gentile leadership experiences inherited by birthright or accession. The leader who ascends through the ranks from tactical to operational to strategic levels of leadership likely had no such benefits, but has dealt with the realities of the good, bad, and ugly in people and organizations. That is why the average person will never pursue leadership. Leaders, their virtues and frailties exposed for all to see, continue to care of their organizations and its people, demonstrating leadership at its finest. That was my Dad. That is why I wrote this book. That is why I want to share why I remain *Inspired, Not Retired*, from leadership or life after all these years.

THE INSIGHT

Instead of simply hanging up my Army officer and leader career after nearly 32 years, I decided to put it to good use in civilian life by continuing to counsel, coach, and mentor leaders at all levels.

As I reflected over my wonderful career, I had outstanding mentors. My noncommissioned officer (NCO) mentors included Master Sergeant John H. Scott, Sergeants Major John W. Quinn, John McCain, Joseph LeStraps, Gary Crecelius, and Old Soldier – SGM Raymond Moran; Command Sergeants Major Randy Bailey, Miguel Ramos, Raymond Moran, and Harold Lewis; First Sergeants Jackie Moore and Danny Crisp.

My officer mentors were Chief Warrant Officer Two Cheryl Jones-Strong; Captain through Colonel Harry G. Simmeth, Jr.; Lieutenant Colonels Armstrong, Nathaniel Field, John Parker, and James Taylor; Lieutenant Colonel and later Colonel Thomas McCool; Colonels Kristen Ellefson and Donald Parker; US Navy Captain Al Davis; Colonel and later Brigadier General Richard McFee; Brigadier Generals John Shortal, John Orr, Henry Huntley, and Gregory Brundidge; Major Generals Vincent Boles and Ronald Johnson; Lieutenant Generals Henry Doctor and Michael D. Rochelle; and General Lloyd Austin.

Even with the enormous number of wonderfully talented and gifted leaders who provided me counseling, coaching, and mentoring along the way, I realized one thing: relatives are your first role models.

Because relatives are in your life from day one, their potential as role models is much greater than anyone else in your life. Your parents, siblings, grandparents, aunts, uncles, and cousins can all influence who you become and how you handle life. I can name almost all my relatives as role models in some way. I spent an ample amount of time with my uncles, Reverend J.B. Randolph, David Randolph, and Calvin Randolph, but I chose to focus on my father, Burl Wesley Randolph, because he was my leader and role model.

THE INSPIRATION

Dad had a solemn expression. The word solemn has many synonyms: earnest, sincere, firm, serious, and grave. But this expression did not truly capture the essence of the man. He was firm but fun, earnest but earthy, and sincere but straight forward. In pictures from his younger days, he held a big, toothy grin. I often hear his hearty laugh in my head, but his sage advice in my soul.

I reflect my dad, who was solemn, but not serious. Let me be clear: Dad could be serious when he needed to be, just like I can, but the solemnness was not always seriousness.

I am uncertain if Dad could be categorized as either an introvert or extrovert, but what I learned over the years was that he was deeply intellectual. Dad read the newspaper, front to back, every day, twice a day, and was conversant on almost any subject of interest to him. I learned this from talking to my four older siblings. Our dad could give advice on just about any subject from A–Z: from attitude to financial independence to working smarter. As a strategic thinker Dad was likely deep in thought about his next move, whether at home or work, with friends, family, finances, on whatever the subject, like going on a fishing trip.

This taught me what it meant to be a self-made man. My Dad only had an 8th grade education, though as the years went on, he gained a bit more—up to the 10th grade! My key takeaway is the old cliché: "Don't judge a book by its cover."

As a senior Army leader, I served with two great officers who I believe were often miscategorized: Lieutenant General (LTG) Michael Rochelle and General (GEN) Lloyd Austin. Whereas most people just characterized them as solemn and/or serious, I found them to be intellectual giants. When others did not understand their guidance and wasted time trying to figure it out, I would simply go ask them for clarification. Remember, earnest but earthy means simple, plain, down-to-earth. Although I am closer in age to both Generals than I was to my Dad – who was 49 when I was born (and I have two younger sisters!), I believe I related to them so well because of my Dad. All three men taught me that doing without thinking is a recipe for disaster.

THE APPLICATION

I will be the first to admit that I can be hard-headed versus hard-hearted. Hard headedness is not an exercise in emotion but in intellectuality. Hard headedness often comes from doing something first without thinking it through. As a leader I have often heard that a bad decision is better than no decision at all. I disagree with that. A bad decision is often simply a decision made too soon and with little insight. Bad decisions have ramifications that cannot always be overlooked through 'buying time.' Bad decisions can have dire consequences and may define the type of leader you are and how others perceive you.

When we retired, Dad and I had completely different lives. Our thought processes diverged on how we came to retire but converged on how retirement made us feel. Below is a comparison of our retirement characteristics for your perusal:

Table 1
Burl Randolph Retirement Characteristics

Characteristics	Burl Randolph	Burl Randolph, Jr.
Age	62	49
Profession	Hi-Lift Operator	Army Officer
Organization	Carter & Water, Inc	US Army
Years Working	27 years, 5 months	31 years, 7 months
Location	Kansas City, MO	Davenport, IA
Retirement Year	1976	2014
Education	Middle School	Masters
Marital Status	Married	Married
# of Children	Seven	Two
Combat	World War II	Desert Shield/Storm Iraqi Freedom x 2

Although we arrived at retire via different paths, there were also a great deal of similarities. We both served in a single organization, retired in the Midwest, had a similar marital status, worked over 25 years, and are both combat veterans.

Two things, however, stand out to me regarding our retirements. First, Dad's perception of retirement after he began it is what colored *my attitude* about retirement. Had things gone differently, I might not have written this book. Second, how Dad lived his life made it possible for me to accomplish what I did in my life.

Dad was my role model. He sacrificed so my siblings and I had the *option* to obtain a higher education if we desired, and maybe most importantly, provided the *opportunity* for us to attend college. I separated these two principles because they do not mean the same thing.

An option is merely a choice to do something, and not all options are opportunities without the means to accomplish them. My siblings and I had the *option* to attend college. Our parents did not require it because part of being an adult is the ability to make decisions for yourself. But it was their hard work and selflessness that provided us the *opportunity* to do so. Leaders not only provide options but opportunities once a decision is made. Without having both the option and opportunity to attend college, I do not know how my life would have turned out.

Because I had never seriously considered retirement at such a young age, knowing when it was time to depart from the first half of my 50-year work [6] life was a difficult decision. Departing the military and then acting on it may be one of my greatest hard-headed moments.

I will not spoil what I have outlined in detail in Chapter Three about knowing when it is time to move on. What I will share with you is this: learn to trust your instincts. Many leadership theorists do not believe instincts play a role in our decision-making processes. I disagree. Sometimes my instincts were all I had when making decisions. The facts did not align, the evidence was circumstantial, and the enemy had cast a vote! In those instances, what I knew from years of experience and felt in the pit of my stomach I adhered to. Our instincts are also sometimes shaded by how we became leaders, which is why retirement is in the eyes of the beholder, and sometimes we shed tears over the event.

Kemper Color Guard was a highlight of my college Freshman year until I became a First Sergeant. I am holding the American flag.

CHAPTER TWO
LEADERS: TAUGHT, BOUGHT, OR SOUGHT?

There is much ballyhoo about leadership.

Yes, I use words that some people have never heard of or much less use, but isn't that what leaders do? They cause you to think differently and help you move to the next level. I did not realize how much ballyhoo there was about leadership until I began to formally study it academically in greater depth. Some people might say there are thousands of leadership models and theories, and they would be incorrect. There are a finite number of leadership models and theories because they were researched, resourced, and written about. But there are likely thousands of opinions about leadership. What I am presenting here is less about my opinion (how I feel about a topic without well-reasoned rationale) and more about my professional assessment (what I believe based on my education and experience).

Some people are sought to be leaders, while others are selected and taught to be leaders. Sought leaders, those selected based on their previous leadership record, are typically bought leaders as well, hired at a premium. The ones who are taught to be leaders may be preselected and groomed for the position based on familial ties or, like me, were members of the military. If I had to pick which type of leader my father was, I would say sought.

In my judgment, a sought leader can also be a person <u>not</u> in a leadership position but *sought* after or acknowledged as a leader by others. Many would say this also describes an informal leader – a person not in a recognized leadership position but who has positive influence over others in the organization. My assessment of my dad is based on knowing him, some things about his life, how he interacted with others, and how he interacted with his family.

Burl Wesley Randolph was born May 21, 1914, the fifth of what would ultimately be 12 children. Although not the oldest male child, Dad was sought as the leader of his family. I can only speculate as to why, but it may have been Dad's determination to succeed and the way he lived his life that inspired change in his siblings.

Dad grew up in and eventually led his family out of a segregated Rural Rison, Arkansas, after serving our country in World War II. He enlisted and served in the famed 10th Cavalry Regiment stationed at Camp Funston, Fort Riley, Kansas. He joined what was then a segregated US military, which may have been his impetus for change.

Even though the teaching of history is a thing of the past (no pun intended), the significance of the 10th Cavalry Regiment is in the adjectives omitted: *All-Black* 10th Cavalry Regiment. The 10th Cavalry was one of four All-Black regiments in the Army. The remaining three regiments were the 9th Cavalry and the 369th and 370th Infantry Regiments. These were not all the units that were 98% Black, with the other 2% of personnel being the White officers who led them.[7] The other units were the 92nd and 93rd Infantry Divisions, the 2nd Cavalry Division, the 4th Cavalry Brigade, the 332nd Expeditionary Operations Group, the 320th Barrage Balloon Battalion, and the 758th and 761st Tank Battalions.

Also, let us not forget the famed Tuskegee Airmen, the All-Black fighter pilot unit in the Army-Air Corps.[8] The sad part about all of this is that the history of Black and African American military units is littered across the internet, with Wikipedia having the most extensive repository. Even our National Archives do not fully capture the service of African Americans during the segregated era in American history.[9] If you care to debate my use of Black versus African American, please see my discussion on this subject in *Mentoring and African American Army Captain Success: A Case Study.*[10]

To my knowledge, Dad was the first to leave the nest through military service, and his siblings soon followed. Once he permanently moved to Kansas City, Missouri, after his discharge from Fort Riley, Kansas, my aunts and uncles departed Arkansas like it was on fire. In the south during the 1940s, this may well have been the case for many African Americans. My point is that some people are sought as leaders whether they pursued the job or not. My father became the patriarch of his family until his death in 1991, which proved a staggering blow to us all. Although sought as a leader by his family, our dad was also sought as a leader at his job.

Having led people all my life, I know the differences between formal and informal leaders. Whereas formal leaders are selected by some authority that places them in the position and may generally be taught leadership principles, informal leaders are selected by the respect they garner from others. This best describes Dad on his job. I don't recall Dad holding a formal leadership position in any organization, but I always observed the respect that was conferred to him. This was most obvious during a company strike in the 1970s.

Although Dad was a card-carrying, monthly meeting member of the very powerful Teamsters Union, when union members went on strike and picketed the company, Dad broke the cardinal rule of the day: he crossed the picket line and went in to work!

There were many organizations striking at that time, and those who walked across the picket line were known as "scabs." Dad would never be referred to by any name other than "Burl." I will explain this later in Chapter 10, Respect.

Scab is not an acronym for anything because in the 70s people used words, not letters, to communicate. Merriam-Webster defines a scab in two ways: The noun version of scab is defined as "a dry, rough protective crust that forms over a cut or wound during healing." The verb is "act or work as a scab[11]." Originally, scabs were known as "strikebreakers." A scab is one of the derogatory terms attributed to someone who crossed the picket line. I am uncertain of this origin for scab, but I would suspect the inference as a coworker who supports the employer by continuing to work, despite the cause that inspired the strike.

Walking across that picket line must have taken great courage. One of Dad's best friends, Mr. Norman, and Dad's younger brother, Uncle David, were his coworkers that went on strike and did not cross the picket line. I do not think "courage" was on Dad's mind at the time.

I asked him, "If you are in the union, why did you cross the picket line?"

He replied "I'm gonna tell you the same thing I told Mr. Norman and your Uncle David when they asked the same thing: I've got nine mouths to feed and bills to pay. I pay my union dues to have them handle this type of stuff."

My question apparently struck a nerve because the conversation did not end there. Dad went on to say that "I also told them that whether we win or lose, I can't afford to not be paid for two or three weeks. You all need to get back to work." I am uncertain, but I think both Mr. Norman and Uncle David did go back to work within the next day or two because they respected Dad and his logic. That is an example of informal leadership at its finest. I imagine that Dad's rationale was that he did not work for the union but worked to feed his family and maintain a living and a lifestyle we had grown accustomed too. The union was a tool which helped achieve that goal, but the goal was accomplished by him working. I believe Dad did not want to cross the picket line, but leaders must sometimes make tough decisions for the good of the organization. In this case that organization was his family, who came first.

THE INSIGHT

Although Dad was in the military, I do not know if he held any leadership positions. Also, as a member of the International Brotherhood of Teamsters, Chauffeurs, Warehousemen and Helpers, Local Union 541, I am unaware of any leadership positions he held with them either. Regardless, Dad was a leader.

As mentioned, leaders can be taught to occupy a position. Some organizations make leadership development a standard practice, and the military is one such organization. Military officers are taught leadership principles throughout the entire Reception, Accession, Development, Assessment, and Retention (RADAR) processes of their careers[12]

There are many ways to learn about leadership through both academic and practical means. Whereas my leadership journey culminated with the scholarly definitions of leadership, Dad's leadership seemed to be from a strictly practical perspective. Some may refer to this as On-the-Job Training or OJT. For many of my clients, OJT means TBF-trial-by-fire. The difference is that while some people naturally gravitate to leadership, others flounder no matter how much academic training or OJT they receive. Again, Dad did not receive any formal leadership training but was always sought as a leader.

This leads us to bought leadership. A bought leader refers to organizational leaders hired for that express purpose: to lead the organization. I once heard an Air Force General say, "The only reason to become a commissioned officer is to lead others." Companies hire Presidents and CEO's to lead organizations into the future. I would posit that all successful military officers are sought, taught, and bought to some degree.

Not all my insights or the accompanying key take-aways (which I refer to as Inspirations) were a quote from my dad. Some, I had to create for myself, such as:

It is not always what you think of yourself as a leader but what those who willingly follow you think of you, that makes you an effective leader.

THE INSPIRATION

To unpack this lesson and develop the Inspiration, the prevailing principle is this: The leader that no one seeks is not a leader, but a figurehead. This thought led me to ponder several questions. How often have you followed someone simply because they were in the position? Have you ever wondered how some people attained leadership positions? Ask yourself some of the following questions to determine if you are a leader. Are you sought, taught, or bought, or simply a figurehead:

1. Do people seek out your tutelage and mentoring?

2. Are you the E.F. Hutton of your group: When you talk, people listen?

3. Are you a Trusted Agent to many, whether you sought the position or not?

4. Do people defer to your judgement, although they may be the expert?

5. Have you never thought of yourself as a leader though everyone else does?

Theories, models, opinions, and definitions do not make leaders. Followers make leaders, and the people who inspire others to serve and perform are leaders. Dad was sought as a leader, and although it may not have been his intention to lead, he got the job done. My desire to lead however, was quite intentional.

THE APPLICATION

Even though this book is about leadership lessons from father to son, other characters will also be introduced to make a point. This leader is my mother, BenElla Randolph. There will be a leadership book about Mom in due time because she had as equal amount of influence on me as my Dad. Mom often spoke in comments that would "get your dander up" to put it lightly. Mom was the one that solidified my desire to pursue leadership in the Army and in life.

I recall explaining to Mom that I had just been appointed to lead an event. Although I do not recollect many of the "pre-dander" comments, I will never forget the rest of the conversation. Mom's response to the news was, "Yep, you always have to be in charge."

Stunned, I replied, "I don't have to always be in charge. I know how to follow!"

"I never said that you did not know how to follow," she replied. "I simply said that you do best, when you are leading."

I stood there, now less stunned and more thoughtful of this new discovery and perspective.

Although I was often sought for leadership, and was frequently taught about leadership, I had to admit to myself that I often pursued leadership opportunities. Consciously or unconsciously, sought or selected, I have always held leadership positions. As the years have gone by and I interacted with extended family members (mostly cousins), I regularly wondered if Dad saw himself as a leader.

Those thoughts occurred to me because my cousins, many significantly older than me, still refer to Dad as Uncle Burl. Titles are a display of reverence, which seem to significantly lack in society today. We should not diminish the people that have earned respect.

One thing I do know that Dad did deliberately: he decided when it was time to stop leading, or at least to stop working. Even in retirement, Dad was still a sought leader.

A young Burl Randolph in his driver's cap, likely in his late 20s following service in World War II.

Dad with Me – Burl Randolph, Jr., around 1965.

Notes Page

CHAPTER THREE
AND THEN, IT WAS OVER

Everyone dreams of retirement, I think.

Retirement makes work in the formal sense, a thing of the past. The *daily grind*, the old *give-and-take*, *the toil*, all phrases used to describe working the J-O-B. Well, I do not believe in retirement at too young an age. This is because it is one of the most difficult transitions in life regardless of when it occurs [13]. When Dad announced he was going to retire I could not believe it! It was around January 1976 and I was in the second semester of the seventh grade. I felt like the Grinch from Dr. Seuss' How the Grinch Stole Christmas: "*Puzzling and puzzling, how could it be so? It came without ribbons. It came without tags. It came without packages, boxes or bags*".

Dad simply announced that he was retiring, and that was it. It was all over. He seemed excited about his decision, and I do not know if he had discussed it with my mom, but I just could not understand it. Dad was only 62 years old. At the time, retirement age was typically 65. My mind raced: "What does he think he's doing? Who retires at 62?" "What is he going to do now?" "What about us?" "How will we live?" The inscription on the back of his retirement watch read: "29 years and five months." Seeing this, I had to ask him, *"You mean you can't do seven more months to get 30 years?* I will never forget his answer:

"When it's time to go, it's time to go".

Although I lived by that principle throughout my nearly 32 years in the Army, I did not and could not aptly apply it when it came time for me to retire. I think it was because I saw what Dad had gone through, how he felt, and the advice he passed on to my brothers and me over the ensuing years. I also remembered that retirement meant starting over.

THE INSIGHT

People may not believe it, but retirement creates a new life. Nothing was the same after Dad retired. He had his retirement party in May, right before his birthday I believe. There was a cake, food, punch, presents, and tons of laughter and joyousness. At least that is what it looked like from the pictures we saw. The company had unexpectedly organized a party, and since it was during school hours, my siblings and I couldn't go.

As an informal or sought leader, Dad was loved and respected by his coworkers and even by the owners of the company. Carter and Water was a construction material firm in the heart of Kansas City, MO. Dad was a '" hi-lift operator'" which apparently is not the same as a forklift operator. After working for that long, in the same position, and being an excellent worker with very few days missed at work, the owners wanted to send Dad out with a bang. I do not recall him being so happy before or after as he was when he retired. His new life began immediately thereafter.

First, Dad drastically altered his wake-up time. Gone was the morning routine of waking Mom at 6:00 am, his personal hygiene at 6:30 am, breakfast at 7:00 am, departing for work at 7:30 am to be at work by 8:00 am. Now he'd awake up at the crack of 8:00 am, saunter to breakfast at 8:30 am, and begin reading his paper by 9:00 am. During the school year, I did not see him until I came home. What a life! We continued our normal routine of yard work, fishing, visiting and the like, but the pace was much slower than before. More relaxed, easy going, and without urgency. Only being around 13 years old at the time, the slower pace was killing me, but I understand now what I could not then:

Know when it is time to go, no matter what position you are in.

Whether you're 22 or 62 it does not matter. When you lose your drive, determination, and/or desire, you are no longer an asset to the organization. You may even be a liability. As I delved further into my Dad's decision to take an '"early retirement'", I discovered that it was well thought out, using many variables most of us ignore. I also discovered that education is not required to be smart. Being smart in this instance meant:

> *If you don't leave when it's time to go, you begin to lose your effectiveness.*

THE INSPIRATION

I realize that I have already made three statements that could be inferred as the Inspiration for this chapter:

A. *"When it's time to go, it's time to go".*

B. *Know when it is time to go, no matter what position you are in.*

C. *If you don't leave when it's time to go, you begin to lose your effectiveness.*

No matter what position you are in or how important you think you are, when it is time to go, it is time to go. Violating this principle can impact your effectiveness in that position. I will explain this painful truth in "The Application".

Always being a Curious Quint, I needed to know the decision-making process Dad used to make this lifechanging choice. Although this is the first time putting this formula on paper, it has swirled in my mind for 37 years – my military career and retired time combined. I always used it, and it always worked, whenever *I* was <u>ready</u> to leave a position. Some considerations for making the decision of when to depart are:

1. **Know <u>what</u> your end goals are**. For every position I ever held, I always knew what I wanted to accomplish, achieved it, and moved on. *Do you know what your end goals are?*

2. **Know <u>when</u> you have accomplished your end goals**. Some people do not establish end goals, so they may always feel like something is unfulfilled. The end goal may be in time, talent, or treasure, but it must be tangible. Dad's end goal had components that I was unaware of. *What is the Measure of Success (MoS) for your end goal?*

3. **Know <u>how</u> you will attain your end goals**. Dad's end goal of treasure had the bonus of time. Dad discovered that a financial incentive was offered for early retirement, so he took it. That was the *treasure* part. Because he retired three years early, he gained more *time* to enjoy retirement. *How will you attain your end goal?*

4. **Know <u>why</u> your end goals, are your end goals**. Although knowing when it's time to go is the premise of the insight and the inspiration, knowing <u>why</u> is even more important. Dad felt that he had given all he needed to all those years by working – physically, mentally, and emotionally. Three

years less wear-and-tear on his body was an additional bonus. *Why is your end goal important?*

As you survey the landscape of your life, what still lives, and what has withered away? I use this poetic prose because writing about work can be mundane. To keep it real and in the right perspective, people do not always have end goals toward retirement, they act like a Nike ad and they "'Just Do It.'" Think of some of the more practical aspects of knowing when it's time to go:

A. **Getting up for work becomes a monumental chore.** Once the job or position loses its luster, no matter how lucrative or important you think it is or you are, it's time to go!

B. **The landscape of the office has changed**. Because people transition in and out of organizations, you are now senior in the company: physically, mentally, emotionally, and in status. You may feel as if you no longer fit in.

C. **You have already attained the maximum amount of monetary incentive you can achieve.** In short, you have maxed out on the pay scale.

D. **There is no more upward mobility.** You cannot be promoted. You have peaked, reached your top, rose to your level of competency (or incompetency).

E. **You cannot make yourself or the organization any better.** Personal and professional growth are important, and if you cannot attain either within the organization, why stay?

F. **Alliances shift.** This one may not be as obvious, but when leaders change, alliances shift, and your top cover may have just bottomed out. If you are now considered bottom sod, not topsoil, it is time to go!

G. **Priorities shift.** What was important when you began, or even just last year, may shift and no longer be important.

You can test these practical aspects against any position, in any organization, to determine from a real-world perspective when it is time to go. Our emotions play a role in all this. Perhaps you're tired of the same-old-same-old, feed-up with your coworkers, expected to do more work for the same pay, and feel the pace of change is too great. Dad had the distinct advantage of meeting all the <u>requirements</u> to retire: the right age, the right years of service, the right amount of savings, and a living wage to retire on. *Do you meet all the requirements to retire? How much longer do you have? Can you see the light at the end of the tunnel, or is it just another train?*

THE APPLICATION

Knowing when it is time to go will save you and possibly the organization the turmoil that eventually ensues from unhappy workers. If any of the scenarios above sound familiar, maybe it is time to consider moving to a new position within the company, moving to a new company, or retiring. There were two instances when I failed to follow a few of the practical aspects of this formula: when I was the Battalion Commander and when I was Brigade Deputy Commander, which are CEO positions in the Army. Both times I extended my tours "'for the good of the unit'" with diminishing returns for myself, my family, and likely my career.

I clearly violated practical aspect E: *Not making myself or the organization any better*. When you are good at something, you believe that it is perpetual. But nothing last forever. I truly believe I was a great Battalion Commander for the first 24 months. The last 12 of the 36 months were some of the most grueling of my career. The unit was highly successful, and everyone wanted to be a part of it. In my first 24 months I only removed through mutual agreement, two Assistant Regional Managers (First Sergeants) and relieved (fired) one. Over the next 10 months, I relieved 11 Assistant Regional Managers, several Branch Managers, and one C-Level officer. This was not good. Because the quantity of removals was so numerous, the focus shifted to *my leadership style* instead of the true reasons.

A successful organization can be a double-edged sword. On the one edge, those who provided the hard work, dedication, and sacrifice to achieve the success can be justifiably proud. On the other edge, the external perceptions of others were that because the organization was successful, any position would be a cakewalk. This is a fallacy, a myth of epic proportions and it almost cost me my career.

In the second example, staying on as the Deputy Commander when all others had fled was also a mistake of epic proportions. You cannot always choose who you work for or with in the Army, and sometimes moving on when you can may be the best action. No matter what I tried, there was little else I could do to improve the unit. Sometimes it is just best to allow people to fail on their own, instead of trying to bail out a sinking ship.

I also failed to consider practical aspect G: *Priorities shift*. When I decided to begin my doctoral program, I should have concurrently submitted my retirement paperwork or at least submitted it a year later. As Dad mentioned, "When it's time to go, it's time to go." I *knew* that I would not be promoted to General Officer. The Army's priorities had shifted, and the Army Chief of Staff guidance had been issued on Colonel-level CEO positions.

Based on that guidance, my window had passed because I was considered too old. Room needed to be made for the new Colonels who were still young enough and hungry enough to sacrifice everything for the Needs of the Army.

Although I thought that I had always served the Needs of the Army, I had not necessarily *sacrificed* to meet those needs. I only had one tour without my family in the 20 years since I had created one. I took advantage of certain Army programs designed to help disadvantaged family members, which kept us together. I rebuffed certain deployment request–Bosnia, because I believed that I had served my time during Desert Shield and Desert Storm. This miscalculation accelerated the retirement process for me. Thank God everything else was in place.

Over the years, part of my duties were promotion notifications. The positive notifications were always fun, and I had no problem allowing the first line supervisors to make the notifications after the big Army announcement was made. Just because the Army released a promotion list did not mean that everyone on the list knew they were promoted. It was one of the better kept secrets in the Army. One of the less pleasant duties was notifying those who were considered but not selected for promotion.

After a couple of emotional nonselective notifications, I decided as the CEO to personally notify everyone not selected for promotion. This is important because people sometimes make split decisions that impact whether they stay until retirement. For some people it was as the title indicated *and then, it was over*. Others had options and opportunities and had weighed those against a hasty departure.

Though many may dream of retirement, it is normally on their terms and in their time. But life surprises you. When it came time for me to make that decision, fortunately, Dad had also instilled in me what most have said is my greatest quality, personally and professionally: patience.

Retirement Luncheon for Burl Randolph from Carter-Waters Corp

Dad (on the right) and unnamed coworker in the
banquet buffet line.

Luncheon banquet table with Dad at the far end.

Mr. Norman (L) and Burl Randolph (R) at
Dad's retirement luncheon

Dad receiving his engraved Bulova watch from
one of the owners.

Dad enjoying coworker comments with Mr. Norman looking on.

An 8th Grade Burl Randolph, Jr. in 1976 at Martin Luther
King, Jr., Junior High School.

Notes Page

CHAPTER FOUR
PATIENCE: A FISHERMAN'S VIRTUE

Sometimes we learn lessons in the oddest ways.

I grew up at a time in society where certain things were still expected of men. In the '60s and '70s the term sportsman encompassed all sports, hunting, and fishing. Young men were encouraged to excel in football, baseball, and/or basketball—the big three—with tennis, softball, and bowling falling in the distant second group. Sports such as golf, volleyball, lacrosse, polo, swimming, and even surfing were considered elite.

Dad loved baseball, and although I tried to emulate his enthusiasm, I just could not do it. I thought of baseball as a strange, awkward little sport that only a certain type of guy played. In truth, I proved to be a strange awkward husky lad that lacked hand-eye coordination to connect the bat with the ball. My size and taste were better suited for football, which Dad seemed to detest, but I played anyway. Hunting was out of the question because the gun laws were much stronger back then. I did, however, excel with a

BB gun once the opportunity availed itself. Fishing became the only option left for us to share.

Dad LOVED fishing. Do you hear me? If Dad could have devoted his life to be a professional fisherman, he would have. But seven kids abated that. I do not recall how often Dad went fishing on Saturdays before I became involved, I just know that it seemed like every Saturday. Soon, I would join him. Dad loved fishing so much he would watch a weekly television show broadcasted in Kansas City entitled *The Sportsman's Friend* anchored by Harold Ensley. Watching the show required total silence, and Dad would practically take notes on which lures to use on what fish, the best times of day to fish, and how to gauge the water.

THE INSIGHT

As you can imagine, back then I had very little interest in the fishing TV show until I began fishing. I am amazed at myself for even remembering these details over 40 years later, but that is how often we watched the show. Dad even watched *The Undersea World of Jacques Cousteau* on Sundays. These details are important because they set the stage for the lesson, which I would learn from spending so much time fishing with Dad:

"Stop fidgeting, or you'll scare the fish!"

In my mind if I heard Dad say that once, I heard it a thousand times. Dad never said anything more than a couple of times however, and then there were consequences. We did what is referred to as still water fishing, contrasted with fly fishing. Still water, as the name implies, means that the water does not move, and neither do you. You are confined to a lake or a pond, rarely a creek or river.

Dad first took me fishing when I was about 8-years old. Can you imagine an 8-year-old sitting still, being quiet, and waiting for a fish that he could not see to attack the bait and swim off? I was not much different than any other 8-year-old boy except that I had a father that loved and spent time with me, and all of us, especially if he could share something he enjoyed.

Envision sitting on dirty, possibly wet ground, on a hard rock, or even standing with a cane pole cast in the water, trying to catch fish. A cane pole is literally a pole made from the reeds of a cane plant, finished and lacquered, and divided into sections which were progressively thinner as the pole extended. This was my first fishing tool and began the second leg of my patience journey.

THE INSPIRATION

You might wonder how one learns patience, but this insight is quite simple:

Be willing to wait for what is important to you.

Patience is simple, especially if you keyed in on the most important words: "willing," "wait," and "important." Spending time with my Dad and catching fish made the willingness easy and also took care of the importance part. The hard part? You guessed it. The waiting.

Waiting is the critical component of patience, regardless of how willing you are or important something is to you. Patience in the little things makes patience in the big things easier. Fishing, required patience for a multitude of tasks:

- Preparing the equipment, the day prior
- Waking up much earlier than normal (sometimes at 2 am)
- Fixing lunch and packing the car
- Traveling to the fishing location (It could be as much as 100 miles away)
- Unpacking the car and distributing equipment
- Walking to the fishing site
- Setting up, baiting, then casting fishing lines
- Then waiting and waiting and waiting

What could we possibly be waiting for now? For the fish to bite. Remember, this is still water fishing, and the fish get a vote! Waiting, looking, and silence were significant but painful for an 8-year-old.

Do any of the fishing tasks look familiar to tasks you are required to complete when preparing for work and your daily life? Think about it for a moment. How much time do we spend in a day waiting for small things?

- The water to warm up in the shower
- The curling iron to heat up (I no longer need one)
- The bacon to finish frying
- Our spouse and kids to respond to something
- In traffic, to and from work
- Our work computer to boot up
- Response to an important email
- Our meals to be cooked or served

Because we must wait numerous times a day for any number of reasons, why are people so impatient? Because they *choose* to be. We will discuss the necessity of impatience later, but impatience is not a virtue that one should aspire too.

What are some of the lessons to becoming patient, or more patient?

1. **Role modeling**. I recall Dad as one of the most patient people I have ever met, so I had a role model to emulate. *Do you have a patient-role model to emulate, or are you that patient-role model?*

2. **Knowing what is important**. If everything is important, then nothing is important. Another consideration is that some things are just not important enough to be impatient over. *What's important to you?*

3. **Humility**. Chapter Five, Humility covers this lesson, but in the meantime, consider this: *Why is what* you *want more important than what someone else wants?*

4. **Critical Thinking**. A wise Command Sergeant Major (CSM) once told me, "Sometimes when you wait or make others wait, the situation may resolve itself". As a Major, CSM Darrell Butler explained to me that sometimes we rush to fix things for others, when others have the solutions themselves.

5. **Creative Thinking**. My wingman, CSM Retired Randy Bailey says, "Sometimes we have to slow down to speed up." When we "rush to judgement' on anything, we may ultimately slowdown the process.

THE APPLICATION

The patience I learned from fishing taught me to be patient in every other facet of my life: school, work, friendships, relationships (some may say otherwise), finances, and in attaining my goals. I have held some of the most critical positions in the Army and in the government, where impatience may have resulted in dire consequences for the organization, me, even the country:

- **Special Weapons Platoon Leader**—High Performance Team (HPT) Leader for tactical nuclear weapons employment team
- **Personal Reliability Program Manager**—Chief Human Resources Officer for all personnel handling tactical nuclear and chemical weapons
- **Battalion Intelligence Officer in Operation Desert Storm**—Vice President for Intelligence and Security
- **Senior Intelligence Officer (SIO)**—C-Level Intelligence Officer in Operation Iraqi Freedom x 2
- **Strategic Arms Reduction Treaty (START) Inspector/Monitor**—Monitored Russian Intercontinental Ballistic Missiles (ICBM) as they exited the production facility

I would be lying if I proclaimed to always be patient, and that I have never been impatient. I also learned from Dad *when* to be impatient.

When we see inequality, social injustices, something that impinges on life, liberty, or the pursuit of happiness, we must be impatient. The doctor directed Dad to go directly to the hospital because of an acute respiratory situation. But our sister Teresa became impatient with our Dad when he wanted to go home first so she drove him and mom directly to the hospital instead.

Suffering from unknown and agonizing pain caused my wife, Terry, to be impatient and she dialed 911. When my son Dominic had an adverse reaction after surgery, I carried him to the car, drove him to the emergency room, carried him inside, and impatiently demanded immediate medical treatment. When a bully attacked our son Derek, we were impatient, and we prosecuted to the full extent of the law.

There are times that demand we be impatient, but not over the trivialities of life. I have experienced the prolonged physical manifestations of impatience resulting in constant and prolonged stress. This may also result in high blood pressure, insomnia, and being isolated because of rude and unacceptable behavior. Just writing this is reflexive and reminds me that I "need not sweat the small stuff" and give people and situations room to grow.

As I mentioned, I learned my lesson about patience in an unlikely manner: fishing. This just proves that patience can be learned by anyone in a myriad of ways. Patience can also assist in gaining humility.

CHAPTER FIVE
HUMILITY: MANNERS MATTER

Respect people for who they are, not what they do.

As harsh as I may come across sometimes, I rarely disrespect people. "Harsh" means to be strict, exacting, tough, and severe.[14] As a career military man, that persona seemed necessary sometimes, but should not define who I am. This aligns with respecting people for who they are, not what they do. Dad may have occasionally been harsh (normally when I needed it), but he was mostly humble. Dad's humility and manners showed because that is how my friends saw him: as a gentleman.

Sometimes we fail to see the best qualities in the people we're closest too. A "gentleman" typically refers to an aristocrat, nobleman, or squire[15] and although Dad did not officially have any of those titles, he appeared that way to my friends. I can remember my friend E.J. Williams saying, "Man, your Dad is just so cool." Our other friend, Michael Roby, said, "Yeh, your Dad just seems like he should come out in a smoking jacket, with a pipe."

Who the heck were they talking about? My Dad? My friend Lonnie Johnson mentioned, "Your Dad always treats us so good when we come over." Lonnie and our late friend James Burton (God rest his soul) were the "we".

THE INSIGHT

Suddenly, I felt ashamed of myself because I looked at my dad for what he *did*, not for who he *was*. I recall him saying, "Just because you live in the ghetto doesn't mean the ghetto should live in you."

Our parents were sticklers for manners. Fail to say, "Excuse me," "Thank you," or "Please" and you learned about the wrath of God by what seemed like a first-hand account! I often heard Dad say, "Beg pardon?" when he did not hear something someone said. What is normally referred to as manners may be derived from humility. I do not ever recall Dad bragging in earnest, and I do not believe that we could brag on ourselves.

Living in a three-bedroom, one-bathroom house with four girls and three boys is where I learned rules, discipline, and manners, not the Army. The girls dressed in private, and the boys dare not look. In our house the boy's bedroom was in the back, which required walking through the girl's bedroom. Everyone had an assigned personal hygiene time in the morning based on when you had to leave for school. Miss your time and go to the back of the line or bribe another sibling to move up!

We all had chores that supported the entire house and opening the driveway gate when Dad drove up from work was one "chore" for the three youngest kids. At first, we silently rebelled, but then it became a contest because occasionally Dad would bring us a treat! I know what you are probably thinking with the gated driveway comment: "Dang, Dr. Randolph grew up la-te-da."

Let's get it straight: "Dr. Randolph" did not exist back then, just plain old Burl, Jr., aka Junior, who had chores like everyone else. We just happened to be blessed with a Dad who liked nice things and provided us a good environment to live in our "gated" yard in the 64130-zip code.

At dinner, we all ate together as best we could, and there were no "seconds" until everyone had "firsts." With only one TV in the house we watched television together. When Dad went to bed, there were hugs, kisses, and goodnights from us younger kids because he went to bed earlier than we did. On the weekends, if you were at home, you helped bring in the groceries and swept and mopped the dining room and kitchen floors. The girls were responsible for indoor maintenance; the boys had outdoor maintenance.

You are likely wondering why all of this is important. I do not believe humility is a natural or innate behavior, but learned from the atmosphere you grow up in. As I have illustrated, my Dad was a man of some stature for that period: a famed Buffalo Soldier military veteran from World War II who had led his family to migrate from one of the poorest areas in Arkansas. He had a well-paying job that supported his large family and held a membership in the Teamsters union. Dad's family and neighbors also respected him. Dad also always seemed to have money. I only write this because when there was a family emergency, the aunts and uncles eventually came to Burl or my cousins referred to Dad as "Uncle Burl". Throughout all of that, Dad just never seemed to puff out his chest and tout his accomplishments.

THE INSPIRATION

How did these insights on humility inspire me?

1. Forced me to look at people versus their property.
2. Kept me focused on the work, not the reward.
3. Allowed me to treat everyone as equals.
4. Instilled a spirit of teamwork versus me work.
5. Eliminated jealousy or envy for what others had.
6. Imparted a spirit of giving.
7. Created a self-deprecating attitude.
8. Implanted the desire to always do my best.

I value the opportunity I had to have humility modeled for me through my parents and older siblings. I saw the Leadership Lesson of Humility modeled daily, so it was easy to learn. Other lessons were not as intuitive and were learned through hard knocks and cold shoulders.

THE APPLICATION

Humility comes in many forms that may benefit you. This application may sound more like a lesson in honesty, but I did not see it that way at the time, or even now. As a young Senior Reserve Officer Training Corps (SROTC) cadet on the land navigation course at Fort Riley, Kansas, I seemed as my oldest sister Lynn Toni would phrase it: directionally challenged.

Global Positioning Systems (GPS) were not something Soldiers had readily available back then, so we were required to be experts at land navigation using a compass, maps, and landmarks. On this day, I had already gone through the course twice: The first time being a team player, I helped a follow Soldier to my demise— he passed the test, and I did not!

I flew solo the second time. Then it happened: I found a wallet stuffed with money and credit cards! At 18 years old and going to be a college sophomore, I had no credit cards let alone significant cash. I did not know the amount of money in the wallet but thought it might make for a great weekend in Junction City, Kansas!

As I stood in front of the drill sergeant grading my paper, I remembered that I had the wallet and handed it to him. "I found it on the trail Drill Sergeant," I said. With the drill sergeant looking through the wallet, a frantic cadet ran in and shouted, *"Did anyone find a wallet?"*

Clearly in a panic and almost beet red, he looked from side-to-side in the tent, searching for the wallet. The Drill Sergeant called him over and barked, "Describe it." The cadet described the wallet, and the Drill Sergeant handed it to him. As the Cadet thanked him profusely, the steely-eyed Drill Sergeant said, "Don't thank me yet. Is it all there?" The Cadet looked through the wallet and almost in tears said, "Yes, drill sergeant, all the credit cards, and all the money: $300."

The Drill Sergeant pointed at me and then said, "Don't thank me, thank him." The cadet shook my hand and said that he owed me a beer. As the drill sergeant continued grading my land navigation course paper, he looked back and forth between me, the paper, and the other cadet. Finally, the Drill Sergeant said, "You passed. Move on to the next station." I have always had doubts about whether I passed the land navigation course unaided.

I do believe, however, that my honesty in not taking anything, and humility in turning the wallet in may have allowed me a mercy not otherwise available. Regardless of how I passed, the humility necessary to turn in the wallet is the point. When we humble ourselves and respect people for who they are, not what they do, good things may come to us. This is especially true when we do bad things, which others pay for.

Class photos from Kemper Military School and College. Left: Freshman year, Fall 1981. Right: Sophomore year, Fall 1982.

SROTC Advance Camp with the fellows at Fort Riley, Kansas before my knee injury.

Notes Page

CHAPTER SIX
PREPAREDNESS: THE ONE P PRINCIPLE

If you travel light, you freeze at night.

Many years ago, I recall the Five P Principle from Colonel John 'Hannibal' Smith, leader of the A-Team, a popular 80s television show. The Five P's are **P**roper **P**lanning **P**revents **P**oor **P**erformance. Although generally true, there are several caveats to that statement:

- "… most of the time."
- "Time passes and weather changes."
- "The enemy gets a vote."

"**Proper planning**" generally increases your odds of success in whatever you do, versus "winging" it.

As I mentioned in Chapter Four, Patience, fishing required a great deal of planning, and my Dad had it down to a science—almost. One special fishing trip threw me off a bit because the usual procedures for the trip changed. The oddity occurred for two reasons: One, only Dad and I were on the trip, and two, we were using a boat! Note I did not write "taking a boat." We had no boat to take. Dad liked simplicity. He didn't own a boat (or yacht), have friends with boats or yachts, nor had membership in a boat or yacht club. We did what everyone else did and rented a boat at the lake. Dad had invested in a small outboard motor, which we used for some time until he upgraded to a Mercury 500. Both motors were kept in the basement next to the sump pump, but on this fine summer day, I noticed the small motor packed for the fishing trip!

Honestly, I do *not* remember much about that day. I do *not* recall the lake we were at, the trip there, or even how we got the boat. However, I *do* recall the former paint cans filled with cement and an eye bolt tied off with rope that looked like clothesline. The paint cans served as our boat anchors, one each for the front and back, or forward and aft as the Navy refers to them. I faintly remember excitedly getting in the boat, and Dad looking at me like I were crazy. He slowly pushed the boat into the water, getting his feet wet as he hopped in. I believe that I should have done that job, since after all, he was the *Captain* of the ship.

I recall us rowing out from the bank a bit and turning the boat around so that Dad could start the motor. Once that puppy started, we were off! As we zoomed into the middle of the lake with the wind on our face, life was great as we navigated a calm water adventure. I had on a life preserver, but of course Dad did not, and I am uncertain why (maybe Dad was more adventurous). But I just know that whatever the safety rules were, I sure had to follow them: seatbelt in the car and life vest in the boat. Unfortunately, we did not wear reflective vests and bike helmets back then, but I am certain if we had, I would have had to wear those too!

It seemed like it took forever but we finally reached our destination: the middle of the lake. With the sun shining, birds were singing, and other boaters were on the water as well. We casted our fishing lines, at least two each, and began the waiting game.

Dad had one side of the boat and I had the other, so as not to get our fishing lines tangled. It seemed like a glorious time until the clouds began to form. The weather began as partly cloudy, then partly sunny, then cloudy with what looked like dark, full pillows ready to burst—and burst they did! It began to rain slowly, and slowly the lesson began.

THE INSIGHT

As I packed up our fishing gear to leave, Dad asked what I was doing.

I said, "It's raining, so we're getting ready to leave, right?"

Dad said, "No, we're not leaving, why would we do that? Just put on your jacket."

Those words clicked in my mind immediately, but my face gave me away when I pulled those Little Orphan Annie saucer eyes.

Dad looked at me, and uttered those fateful words: "Where's your jacket?"

I could not think of anything to say to make it better or change the situation. I simply said, "I didn't bring it." I did not say that I forgot it, or I misplaced it, I merely told the truth, I did not bring my jacket.

The next words from Dad were, "You need to always be prepared when you are on the water." This paled in comparison to his actions: He took his jacket off and handed it to me.

After he told me to put it on, he then said, "Pull up the anchors." The rain really pelted us as we prepared to return to shore, and with our father-son outing ending, I felt like I had ruined the trip. Dad started the engine, which seemed to take forever, turned the boat around, and headed for the bank. As we raced in, we did not talk. I would not have been able to hear him anyway over the roar of the rain and the engine. I felt sad and lonely on the boat ride in.

When we got to the shore, I instinctively jumped into the water and pulled the boat in. With Dad being soaked, getting my feet and legs wet were a minor inconvenience. It's times like these we learn the virtue of a parent's patience. He looked a little surprised, a much better expression than the angry look he had worn just five minutes earlier when he handed me his jacket. I literally did the heavy lifting by taking the anchors back to the car. Even though I made several trips, I carried all the equipment while Dad took off the motor and pulled the boat all the way in. I realized that there must have been some modicum of trust left when he gave me the keys to the car. I no longer felt disowned.

THE INSPIRATION

I have no memory of any conversation on the way home, nor what I said when my mom asked how we did with the fishing. I think Dad just said that we got rained out. This inspiration has stayed with me all these years:

Always be prepared

Not always be ready, willing, and able, but always prepared for whatever it is you are doing or about to do. Many believe I was a Boy Scout, or I gained that from my military training, but neither assessment would be true. I learned this lesson from the "School of Hard Knocks," and let me tell you, it has some brutal teachers.

No Army captain, colonel, or general taught me this lesson, because they were never given the chance. I learned this lesson from someone I respected and admired long before and after I joined the military, my Dad.

What does always be prepared mean?

1. **Think critically about the task and what is needed to complete it**. This means thinking through what the task is, what is required for success, and making certain that you are postured for success. Writing a list of the requirements helps tremendously.

2. **Think creatively about the nuances of that task.** Even if you have done the task a hundred times before. I had packed the car for our fishing trips weekly during the spring and summer for years, but not for a *boating* trip.

3. **When the task seems different, ask questions**. My excitement overshadowed my normally curious self, so I did not ask the Who, What, Where, When, Why, and How that I have come to annoy people with over the years.

4. **Double-check yourself, and even triple-check with the team.** I learned the value of checking from every deployment to the National Training Center (NTC), to Iraq, to Germany (the Grafenwöhr and Hoenfels Training Centers in Germany), to Russia, to Iraq, and back to Iraq

again. Checking may be annoying but forgetting something may be catastrophic.

5. **Sometimes we must insist**. There will be times that you check, and people will intentionally not pack necessary equipment. As the leader, sometimes you must overrule their judgement and insist they pack all the items on the packing list.

Whether it is packing shelter halves when going out for field training, packing General Purpose (GP) small tents for pre-deployment training, or packing cold weather gear on deployments to Iraq, one thing is certain:

If you travel light, you'll freeze at night.

This statement may *not* be as true today, in the era of poly pro and under-armor gear, but the lesson of preparation remains relevant. I can attribute preparation as a critical element of my success in my educational pursuits, my military career, and the doctoral program.

THE APPLICATION

Everyone wants to be remembered for something. However, infamy is not a positive trait. As we, my Army unit, completed reorganizing the entire military intelligence (MI) battalion from *functional intelligence disciplines* (Signals Intelligence (SIGINT), human intelligence (HUMINT), and electronic intelligence (ELINT)) *to multidiscipline intelligence companies*, the struggle was real. Integrating three different specialties from three different companies into three new but like companies became arduous. Then came the real test: Combat Training Center (CTC) deployment.

CTC deployments were the pinnacle of training in Germany. Each maneuver battalion (infantry, armor, aviation) from a selected maneuver brigade (three battalions, a headquarters, and supporting elements) rotated into the CTC and then out in two-week increments. The MI units were not so fortunate. The MI company that supported that brigade deployed for six weeks. Because these deployments were so long without returning to the base, having the necessary equipment was essential.

The ELINT teams resisted taking all the equipment on the packing lists because "We don't use tents and camouflage nets... and we are used to doing it our way." Instead of me saying, "That may be true, but now you are going to do it my way," I simply said, "Humor your new company commander and pack your tents and camouflage nets. Who knows? They may come in handy." Long story short, 1995 may have been the rainiest October in German history up to that time, or at least it felt like it. Unexpectantly, I required the ELINT teams to convert from training exercise mode into a real-world mission: Search and Rescue.

On this day, no one had heard from the infantry scouts (the forward lookouts who detect and observe the enemy, but do not engage) for more than six hours. The torrential downpours made it impossible to send out additional search parties. Because my ELINT teams were all accounted for, safe and secure inside their nice, dry tents, I volunteered their services to find the scouts. By activating the listening equipment, they could distinguish between human and equipment sounds versus the natural sound of the rain. Consequently, the two scout teams were found within an hour: one team was wet but alright and the other team suffered from mild hypothermia from being cold and wet for so long.

After we returned from the field, the ELINT Team Chief said, "Thanks sir." I said, "For what?" and he replied, "For not *ordering* us to take the tents and camo but insisting. You were really looking out for our safety." After that rotation, all ELINT teams throughout the battalion (corporation) routinely packed their tents and camouflage nets as required by the packing list. The significance of this detail? The habit became a necessity when the battalion deployed 14 months later to Bosnia for peace keeping duty. The terrain in Bosnia mirrored Germany, so the unit benefitted greatly from the training and preparation. Although I did not deploy, I knew in my heart that I had prepared my unit for the task at hand because Dad had prepared me as a planner. Dad also taught me that being considerate of others is just as important as planning.

Me as a Company Commander, A Company (Collection and Jamming), 501st Military Intelligence Battalion, Dexheim, Germany, Sep 1995 – Sep 1996.

First Sergeant Jackie Moore handing me my first challenge at the Change of Command Party, Sep 1995.

Winners, A Company, 501st Military Intelligence Battalion Organization Day, 1995.

CHAPTER SEVEN
SELFLESSNESS: BEING CONSIDERATE

It's not always about you.

As you may have guessed, my dad enjoyed life. Hunting, fishing, time with family, napping, etc., were some of his favorites. The one pastime that taught me something and that we could also enjoy together was watching TV. I grew up in an era of black and white televisions with rabbit ear antenna and no remote control. Homes did not have cable TV or Dish with normally only one TV per household. If you had money, there may be more than one TV in the house, or perhaps a satellite dish in the yard as big as the space station. In the 70s, technology continued to evolve, so electronics were big. I also had a big appetite, and my lessons in manners and humility had obviously not sunk in.

THE INSIGHT

Dad enjoyed watching westerns. Baseball, fishing, and westerns were the three types of programs that I knew Dad liked, although years later in retirement, his horizons expanded. On this Saturday, the kids show I watched concluded and a western followed, so I got up to leave.

"Oh no you don't. Where do you think you're going?" said dad.

"To play," I replied.

"Why?" said dad (oh no, the dreaded why question!).

"Because I don't want to watch this show," I said.

"It's not always about what you want," said dad. "I sat here and watched your show and didn't say a word, so the least you can do is watch mine. And you're gonna watch it!"

I do not recall the show, maybe *Hop-A-long Cassidy* or something like that. If it were, I would have just taken the punishment instead. Whatever the western, we watched it together, dad explained things to me, and I enjoyed it. I have enjoyed westerns ever since, and they are one of my favorite movie genres.

Dad could have allowed me to just walk away and do my own thing, but he did not. He taught me how to be considerate: thoughtful, kind, understanding, selfless. As a child of eight or nine, I knew what I liked but did not have the maturity to appreciate what others valued.

THE INSPIRATION

Being self-reflective and honest I can truly say that I have not always been considerate in the traditional sense of thoughtful and understanding. I have strived to be kind and selfless, but guess what? It is a package deal. In my opinion, all these attributes – thoughtful, kind, and understanding—work together to help a person become selfless. At least that is the way it worked for me. The incident with Dad did make me more aware of other people's feelings, but it did not create what Daniel Goleman considered Emotional Intelligence (EI).[16]

I describe EI as the intersection of acknowledging one's emotions and intelligence, and to express those emotions in a thoughtful manner while being cognizant of other people's feelings and disposition. The reason I used the word thoughtful versus controlled as in the original definition is because attempting to control one's emotions is easier said than done. Remember this when you read Chapter Nineteen, "Compassion and Loyalty"

Being thoughtful is an external action that requires placing other people first. To place other people first requires you to place your feelings second or lower. To be considerate in this way takes a great deal of discipline versus control. I am not saying that EI is easy, but I am saying that acknowledging our own feelings, other people's feelings, and thinking through how to balance the two is challenging.

Some things to ponder about being considerate that can lead to selflessness:

1. Is what's important to you important to others?
2. Is what's important to others important to you?
3. Are you willing to place your wants, needs, and desires second to someone else's?
4. Who comes first, you or the organization? Your family?
5. Is what you are giving up a sacrifice?
6. Will your sacrifice make someone else happy?
7. Can you sacrifice and not feel bitterness or regret?
8. Can you find joy in helping others?
9. Do you have the discipline to control your emotions?
10. Can you relinquish control to others?

I am certain this all sounds foreign to some readers and is a little unsettling to me because I have never seen myself like this. Truth be told, selflessness is one of many qualities that made me successful as a leader. It also gained me friendships.

THE APPLICATION

I have always been a man in uniform. Not as a Cub Scout or Boy Scout, or on an intermural sports team, nor did I march in a band. In the sixth grade, however, I served on a coveted position with the elementary School Safety Patrol. Yes, I had a life before the military! I chose this story because one does not become considerate overnight. In my mind, consideration is a product of when opportunity meets sacrifice and, in this story, I really sacrificed.

We had finally made it: upper classmen in charge of the School Safety Patrol. Each sixth-grade class held the mantle of responsibility for one month and had the opportunity to receive rewards and prizes for exemplary performance of duty. Okay, we were kids. A snickers candy bar would have been a great reward but at least we were recognized!

For those of you who have no clue what I am talking about, the School Safety Patrol is the precursor to the modern-day School Crossing Guard position filled by adults. Back in my day (I have always wanted to say that!), the school crossing positions were manned by students taking care of other students. A teacher assisted as over-watch, but the students had it going on, helping the younger kids to obey the traffic lights and signs, safely cross the street, and instill good order and discipline in drivers. Okay, that last part was a stretch but the rest of it occurred!

Our class finally had the duty in October of that year, and the teacher selected Darnell as the Patrol Lieutenant. The Lieutenant's responsibilities were developing the schedule, assigning the positions, and most importantly, selecting someone as Sergeant to enforce standards. Guess who Darnell selected? That's right, me! At that time, I relished being the Enforcer because it alleviated me from doing the paperwork and coordinating with the teachers. My job was to make certain that everyone else did as they were instructed, fill in gaps as needed, and resolve any conflicts.

To tell you the importance of school safety patrol, each class had a ceremony to swear in the new safety force! We had badges and orange Sam Browne-type belts, one around the waist and one diagonal across the body. We also had cards with our names on them identifying us as Safety Patrol when we were off duty.

I know this all sounds hilarious to an adult, but when you are a child, any opportunity to have authority was a great honor and very exciting. However, my best friend Lionel came to me with fear in his eyes. That curtailed my excitement.

"Burl, you can't take the sergeant's position," he said, nearly in tears.

"Why not Lionel? Aren't you happy for me?" I asked.

"Burl, you don't understand," said Lionel. "I don't trust Bobby. He's mean! When we are alone, and he hits me. A lot. I know he will."

Before I could say anything, Lionel used the Kid's Kryptonite on me and said, "*Please*, Burl, be my patrol partner."

Lionel was my best friend after-all, and we had clicked from the moment we met. I knew what I had to do to help my friend.

I went back to Darnell and told him that I would stay on patrol and wanted to be partnered with Lionel. Oh, you just do not know how it pained me to do that. I had already been sworn in as the sergeant and the announcement had been made. Worse yet, I already had the SERGEANT badge, which had a green background. The LIEUTENANT badge had a blue background and PATROL had no background. This felt like a lot to give up for friendship and to assuage someone else's fears, but all I could think of is what Dad had said: "It's not always about you." We made the swap, and I went back to curbside duty with Lionel. Kids can be very intuitive, and as the saying goes, "No good deed goes unpunished."

Darnell selected Bobby as the new Sergeant, which should not have mattered. Apparently, Bobby figured out that Lionel did not want to be partnered with him and became slightly vengeful. The next day the duty roster changed, and Lionel and I went from the premier patrol post helping fellow students at the crosswalks, to the most remote safety post in the school. We were reassigned to the playground back doors!

Oh, how the mighty had fallen! I could not believe it! The bright spot? Being an elementary school in Kansas City, Missouri in October, there were no outdoor activities on the playground after school! While kids could exit from that door, no one could come in. The door locked after it closed and outside personnel could not reenter, and we were forbidden from letting them in. Our tour of duty ended when the janitor or security guard came by and put chains on the door. Or so we thought.

As we were about to pack it in, Bobby popped up. "And where do you two think you're going?" he asked.

"Home," I said. "The doors are locked so we are done, right?"

My fatal mistake? Asking if we were done. I have adhered to the cliché that "It is better to beg forgiveness than ask permission" ever since.

"No, you're not done. Get back to your positions until four thirty," Bobby barked.

Four thirty? A full hour after school ended. Why did we need to look at locked doors for about 30 minutes? It really burned Lionel and I the first couple of days, but we noted the immense pleasure Bobby derived from that. When Bobby came the third day, we pretended our doors were the most important safety patrol post in the school and requested reinforcements! This did not amuse Bobby but then, the Vice Principal suddenly appeared.

"What are you boys doing here?" he asked.

"We're on Safety Patrol," we responded.

Puzzled, he asked, "Why are you guarding chained doors?"

"Because the Sergeant told us too," said Lionel.

"We'll see about this tomorrow," said the VP.

Because we guarded the back door, we were only on shift after school. We arrived in class just in time to see Darnell strip Bobby of his Sergeant's badge! Darnell offered the position to me again, but I declined. Just like in the cowboy shows, I enjoyed my time partnering with Lionel although it was not my first choice.

Lionel and I were reassigned back to the premier patrol position. And Bobby? He was stuck on the playground back door, alone!

I used this example because if I could learn consideration of others and selflessness as a child, applying the principle as a Soldier, officer, husband, father, and leader came with less effort. Less effort, however, did not mean painless.

Mom and Dad having fun after the Saber presentation ceremony.

Notes Page

CHAPTER EIGHT
HARD WORK: IT WON'T KILL YOU

Really, hard work won't kill you.

Hard work has made America great. Yes, intelligence, ingenuity, and innovation were all part of the equation, but they all required hard work to reach fruition. My parents worked hard in and outside of the home. As I mentioned before, Dad was a hi-lift operator and Mom was a domestic engineer. Mom did not play when it came to her responsibilities, so the phrase stay-at-home mom did not fly. Getting eight people out of the house before 8 am after cooking breakfast and preparing various lunches was no easy chore, and Mom let us know it. That is the type of hard work that I am talking about that likely occurred in most households across America during that era. For me, Dad had a different vision of hard work.

THE INSIGHT

All of the outside chores were mine, plain and simple. This involved cutting grass, washing the car, plowing the garden, deseeding the garden, shoveling snow, pruning trees, and whatever else Dad thought of. As I became older, my duties expanded to changing siding, replacing shingles on the roof, sharpening tools, helping with oil changes, replacing storm windows, chalking the seams around windows, harvesting vegetables from the garden, and "making things," which will be covered in a Chapter 21-Creativity.

Additionally, my inside duties consisted of taking out the garbage nightly, taking trash to the curb weekly, washing dishes, mopping floors, and bringing in the groceries. Now, I do not want to misrepresent my requirements. ALL my siblings had chores distributed at various levels. Once my older brothers departed, however, all outside tasks fell to me. I had some consternation about that, but Dad cleared that up.

THE INSPIRATION

Some things are better left unsaid. I believe I made a comment about "having to do everything," to which Dad responded, "Hard work won't kill you." It sure felt like it was going to kill me. It was the summer, and I was stuck in the kitchen doing dishes, after I had just cut the entire yard. Dad must have felt sorry for me or something and mentioned to Mom that my dishwashing career was over. Not one to back down, Mom asked, "Why?" A lively discussion ensued. I continued washing dishes because I knew that I was not off the hook yet. Mom argued that my inside chores were life skills that I needed, and Dad countered by saying that my sisters would now be required to cut grass and shovel snow because those were life skills also.

Mom vehemently opposed my younger sisters doing outside chores but understood Dad's point. Since I had been doing those life skills chores for so long, Mom surmised that I may have mastered them. The inside chores decreased as the outside chores increased, but what I had already learned from both experiences could not be taken away. My hard work in and outside the house would be the foundation for my success in college, in the Army, and as an adult. Although I have already learned the answers through experience, I still ponder certain questions:

1. Could I have been successful without hard work?
2. Is hard work a life skill missing today?
3. Is hard work a cornerstone of leadership?
4. Does hard work diminish as one ascends the leadership ladder?
5. Is there ever an exemption from hard work?

Because we all learn in different manners, what may come easy to others requires hard work by some. I have always had to work hard to not only achieve what I wanted, but sometimes just to be average.

I can remember having homework in the first grade. Yes, that's right, the first grade. One hour of reading nightly to a parent. Being a slow reader has occurred my entire life. Because of not meeting the "speed of reading" benchmark, I received additional attention and instruction. Funny thing is, although I have always been a slow reader, my comprehension skills are off the charts! I have observed that reading quickly but not remembering or understanding what you read is not beneficial. Reading quicker is hard work for me and required hard work to improve. I do not believe I have mastered that skill yet.

In the third grade I had difficulties in math. Once again, one hour of math problem solving homework nightly with a parent. This occurred until I reached the math benchmark.

Fourth grade brought my first academic accolades. As a child, I *thought* perfect attendance and good citizenship awards were for what I accomplished. Those awards were more attributable to good parenting, so I do not count those as academic achievements. I received awards in Language Arts (English), Math, and Science. Obtaining those awards required hard work when you are not a naturally gifted student. I could regale you with homework, tutoring, and remedial stories abound, but the point is that my early academic successes were obtained through hard work.

Even though success is defined by the person, those areas in which I excelled required hard work. Sometimes I forgot, however, that hard work has no rank or position and pays no homage to race or gender.

THE APPLICATION

Throughout the military services there is a common saying among noncommissioned officers when referred to as Sir or Ma'am: "Don't call me Sir (or Ma'am). I work for a living."

There is no dispute that the physical labor conducted in the Army is completed by the enlisted corps, led by Non-commissioned Officers (NCO). NCOs are the backbone of the Army and the US military. They are key to our successes. Enlisted service members outnumber officers by three to one because of the vital roles they play in the organization. Our enlisted corps are so proficient, we sometimes take their contributions for granted.

During Operation Iraqi Freedom One, coalition liaison teams were formed to help coordinate with our allies. Because of my intelligence specialty, I became the unit intelligence officer after the initial training. When training resumed, I added in the intelligence flavor through developing vignettes, evaluating performance, and issuing intelligence updates. After training ended and with deployment imminent, my focus turned to preparing myself, preparing my family for my departure, and preparing intelligence for the organization.

My family and I were moving from one townhouse to another because the one we rented was sold but fortunately, we were just moving next door. My sons, Dominic and Derek, were five and two at the time, so my wife Terry watched them in between packing. I packed, moved things over, came back, and repeated this routine for at least a week. I hired a moving company to move all the heavy furniture—couches, beds, German shrunk, grandfather clock, etc.—for that Saturday. The weather forecast predicted heavy snow beginning Saturday at noon, and oddly enough, the predictions were correct!

It began snowing precisely at noon, the movers had just completed their part, and everything occurred smoothly, right? Wrong! We were scheduled to depart for Iraq on Sunday, but the snow had become a blizzard, closed the roads and airports in Maryland, Virginia, and Washington, DC, and did not stop until sometime on Monday. By the way, we were still scheduled to deploy. What is the point of this passage? Although moving does involve some planning skills, the physical act of moving requires heavy lifting, and heavy lifting is hard work.

Because we were still scheduled to deploy, we assembled at the Army base for headcount, loaded our equipment on the buses, and made our way to the Air Force base, all in 12-plus inches of snow. We were notified on the bus that all flights were grounded, and we were diverted to a nearby hotel that had already closed, but since the storm had stranded the hotel nightshift, they opened for us. We had to unload the buses in the snow, move the equipment into the hotel, and develop a security plan for the weapons and such. This all required hard work. The weather cleared up by Tuesday, and we finally departed on Wednesday. With more hard work, we did finally arrive in country to conduct our mission.

As with any military mission, accounting for the basics is a normal task. One basic is force protection. Force protection represents a series of tasks required to keep the force safe and secure from enemy activities. This may mean keeping your chemical protective suit nearby, your weapon loaded with ammunition but on "safe," and keeping abreast of enemy activities.

These are tasks that all service members can and do perform. However, there are some tasks in the Army that only junior enlisted Soldiers perform. Those included guard duty, convoy security, and preparing fighting positions. A fighting position is a fortification that keeps you safe from enemy fire and is commonly referred to as a "foxhole." Fighting in Iraq had uncommon circumstances, and foxholes were not always practical.

Because of the pace of combat operations, an unconventional enemy, and the sandy terrain, sandbag fortifications were more common. What happened next brought me back down to earth.

Our Senior Enlisted Leader, First Sergeant (1SG) Ronkin, entered the operations center to make an announcement. This uncharacteristic move by him caught our interest, so when he said that he needed our attention, we listened, especially the way he said it.

"Gentlemen," he began, "we need to fill sandbags to build fighting positions. Based on the way we are organized; I don't have enough junior enlisted to fill sandbags and complete all the other requirements."

What he said next was the kicker.

"If you officers want fighting positions, you're gonna have to fill your own sandbags."

We all looked at each other with the "Did he just say that?" look on our faces. Before we could even react the O-6, Colonel Smith echoed, "You heard him, so you Majors need to grab some shovels."

At this point I'm thinking that everyone had gone crazy! Still being a Major, filling sandbags included me. As I filled sandbags I muttered under my breath, "When I get promoted to Lieutenant Colonel, I'm not filling another sandbag!"

I was in a pissy mood until my promotion four days later. After my promotion, filling sandbags would be a thing of the past. As a Lieutenant Colonel, I vowed to never fill another sandbag. In fact, my duties became even more critical: I held the sandbags as the Major's filled them!

No one made me do this, but as I now *observed* sandbags being filled, I recalled the difficulty in filling a sandbag alone. After I "pitched in" the task became more manageable.

Some might say that the Majors could have double-teamed this all along. Working 16-hour days on different shifts however, made that impossible. The Majors were not just subordinate to me, but also my comrades and friends.

Combat brings a closeness because of shared vision, values, and goals. Rank does not dilute that. A year later when I assumed Recruiting Battalion Command (Chief Executive Officer), I always told this story during New Recruiter Orientation to empathize a point: Leaders do what is required to accomplish the mission … Even if it is not part of their normal duties!

Filling sandbags was hard work and not beyond my abilities or responsibilities as a leader. As a Recruiting CEO, making phone calls, talking to applicants, or scheduling the Armed Services Vocational Aptitude Battery (ASVAB) test for applicants were not my responsibilities, but were also not beyond my capabilities. Yes, those were all basic Recruiter duties. The Station Commanders or Regional Leadership Teams were not required to conduct those duties either, but in a pinch, leaders do what is necessary to posture for success.

As I discovered about every accomplishment in my life, hard work was a cornerstone and it did not kill me. There were times when I thought hard work might kill me: keeping my weight down for 32 years to stay in uniform, earning each college degree, serving in combat, and in Army recruiting. I am accustomed to hard work, and had it not been instilled in me by my parents, I am uncertain where I would be. Although Dad did not make hard work fun, he did make it palatable, understandable, and necessary to carry on the Randolph name. Dad also made intellect a necessity to accompany the hard work. Now I can pass this advice on to my sons. Hard work won't kill you!

Another parade. From L to R: John SP Lizama, Terence Hoppe, Patrick Lenz, and Mahalani Akina. Spring Semester, 1983. College Battalion Staff.

CHAPTER NINE
INITIATIVE: FIGURE IT OUT

Initiative is a key to self-development.

I have always been a tinkerer. I had a chemistry set and conducted experiments in my bedroom. I took things apart and put them back together with excess parts at the end. This required me to strip, rebuild, use all the parts, and test drive the item. My time as a model car builder was fleeting (not enough patience). I attempted to play several instruments, but that gene skipped my generation, or at least me.

With some instruction from Dad, I became quite handy with tools and even built myself a table in my bedroom. Although not aesthetically pleasing but functional, it served me until I left for college. I suspect my parents jointly took it apart and distributed the wood in a way that I could not find it for reassembly. My inquisitive nature would be both a blessing and a curse as I became older and had more responsibilities.

THE INSIGHT

My tinkering extended to my schoolwork as well. Back then George Washington Carver fascinated me by his more than 300 uses for the peanut.[17] [18] I had decided to become a scientist (hence the chemistry set), but of course back then I was also a "jack-of-all-trades-and-master-of-none." Because of my longstanding family recognition as the Nutty Professor, my Dad decided to capitalize on my skills.

First, we assembled a barbeque grill together. We transitioned from the cheap, three-legged grill that had limited cooking space, only got hot in the middle, and everyone else in the neighborhood had one, to a real man's grill.

We assembled and placed the new Char-Broil grill into use, and it served our family faithfully for years. I am certain that there were several other little put-this-together projects in between, but I cut my teeth on this special one.

I recall this special project because I was awakened on a Saturday to execute it. I staggered into the living room, blurry-eyed and still half asleep (No, I was not intoxicated at nine or 10 years old!). With a huge box in the middle of the room with a picture of a lawn mower on the side, Dad appeared excited. He seemed to think that I should be just as excited. All I could think was, "Huh, just more ways to do work." We opened the box and began taking out the parts. Then we lifted the frame out of the box, and I said, "Okay, what's next?"

I found Dad's response odd: "*You figure it out.*"

With that comment I became fully awake. Dad said it and strolled away to leave me to my own devices. Assembling barbeque grills and small power tools was one thing, but a lawn mower? Especially after my older brother Larry had a lawn mower accident that haunts me even today. So, dad wanted me to assemble this toe eating machine? (Yes, I can be quite dramatic in my mind for someone so cool, calm, and collected on the outside.) With the order given, and I had no place else to live, I figured that I should earn my keep and comply.

THE INSPIRATION

With this new experience I began with something I rarely did-I retrieved the assembly instructions. This departed from the finest male tradition of ignoring instructions as a part of the assembly process. I violated the "bro-code" and read the instructions. I know, the horror of it all! However, in this instance, I took no chances.

After assembling a lawn mower in the living room, which made Mom quite unhappy, I needed to test drive it. I challenged my father on this, smoothing it over by saying the "honor" of the first pull should be his. It didn't work, and he had me push it outside and fire it up.

The lawn mower had no gas, so I had to go through the normal motions of preparing it for operations. After 15 minutes of mowing, without the wheels, blade, and blade guard falling off, Dad took over.

After that opportunity, I assembled other things with little to no supervision or apprehension, such as a rotary tiller. This experience created initiative in me. I no longer needed someone to give me instruction, supervision, or permission to do certain things, I just did them.

I interact with numerous business leaders and one of their main concerns is developing initiative in the workforce. I believe initiative is vital for both leaders and workers. When training leaders, I use what I refer to as the "Three 'No' Criteria in Developing Initiative":

- No instruction
- No supervision
- No permissions

Sometimes as leaders, I believe we fail to create the conditions that create initiative. Therefore, leaders must ask themselves several questions:

1. **What <u>guidance</u> have I given?** Prior to Dad telling me to "figure it out," he provided instruction, guidance, and practical application before the training wheels were taken off. *Have you provided any instructions or guidance on how* you *want things done in your organization?*

2. **What supervision have I provided?** Again, the only person surprised when Dad stopped supervising me, was me. *Have you provided supervision? If, so, what was the quality of the supervision? How long did you provide supervision? Have you ever stopped providing supervision?*

3. **What permissions have I granted?** I believe that granting permissions is one of the most difficult criteria for many leaders. When we assign, delegate, or hold people accountable, we have granted permission. Granting permission means vesting our power and authority into someone else, which requires another quality: trust. *What permissions have you granted? Who have you granted permissions too? Are you delegating or micromanaging? Are you blaming without building? Who do you trust?*

4. **Is initiative rewarded or reprimanded?** Some leaders who have control or power issues do not welcome initiative, so there is no reward for doing more or doing things without being asked. In extreme cases, initiative is

reprimanded to discourage resourcefulness and maintain control of the individual and the situation. *How is initiative rewarded? Is initiative a discriminator or detractor in performance evaluations?*

5. **Is initiative valued in your leaders?** Initiative is a key trait of self-starters. Leaders must be self-starters to move forward, even when the chips are down. *If leaders are held to a higher standard, is initiative one of those standards? Is initiative valued in your organization?*

Guidance, supervision, permissions, reward, and value are the Initiative Indicators we should all look for to determine how our initiative will be received. Always being rewarded for my initiative motivated me to pursue it in all facets of my life. Initiative sometimes means taking off your own training wheels, figuring things out yourself, and learning to ride solo. Initiative, however, does not always work out the way you think.

THE APPLICATION

As much as I like writing, it's hard work, especially when you are doing it for someone else. So far, all my Applications have been military, or leadership related. Initiative, however, is often about getting the work done. I helped write *Can God Trust You with Trouble?* while in the second year of my doctoral studies and had written extensively. Let me define extensively. Ten writing assignments a week to include a 10 plus page paper on a research topic directed by the instructor. The writing evaluation included all aspects of grammar, but most of all, content. I have read books, magazines, essays, blogs, and all manner of literary papers that met all aspects of the King's English. However, they left me wanting and wondering for substance. Each of these more than 500 writing assignments were assessed with a grade. That is how I define extensive.

Although I said that writing is hard, try editing. I have only edited my own work one time and when I looked back at it, I cringed. Writing and editing are two different skills sets and should be given the appropriate respect for those who excel at one or the other. Then there is publishing, which may be considered another task in the writing genre. In fact, it is not. Publishing is part of the literary chain: writing, editing, publishing, promoting, and selling. Although you can pay a company or person to complete every element in this literary chain, the self-publishing industry has become very prolific for those who wish to control their own destiny at a fraction of the costs.

While helping write the Trust You with Trouble book, I also wrote my own peer-reviewed article, "Changing Steps: A Reflective Journey in Transition." My publisher, *The Journal of Global Health Care Systems*, handled all the publishing duties, so the complexities involved did not occur to me. When the Trust You with Trouble book's primary author mentioned publishing through a system named CreateSpace (now Kindle Direct Publishing (KDP)), I jumped on the task. I showed initiative, though not all the Initiative Indicators were present or even possible, which made my job much harder.

I followed the guidance to use CreateSpace for publishing. Neither of us had ever used it before, so no supervision occurred. Figuring it out is what I am best at, right? I figured it out through trial, error, extensive time, and great pain. Considerations like book size—standard or custom, page texture—white versus creme, and cover design were all decisions for the author based on recommendations from me. The more technical aspects of templating, page bleed, and spine type were not intuitive in any way and no recommendations could be made, so once again I flew solo.

Permissions—account ownership became the most complicated aspect. With KDP, whoever owns the account basically owns the book, regardless of who the author is. This includes the basic and technical considerations of publishing, but also the benefits of promotional help and most importantly, sales. There must be a bank account linked to provide royalty checks, which is an aspect of tracking sales. Reordering books, where to ship them, and the timing of book publication versus events are also considerations. A prudent businessperson does not want to have an exorbitant number of books on hand but can reorder when needed. The last aspect of permissions is that there can only be one person on the account, and to change it would mean disrupting availability of the book.

Although things have worked out from that initial experience, I learned the tasks required for publishing and became better equipped for my next client. The experience also allowed me to consult on self-publishing from a practitioner perspective. There is nothing quite like figuring things out on your own, even with all the literature, consultants, and expertise available. Even with great initiative, it does not replace other aspects of your personality, if people or a person sees you in a different light.

My first major project after starting MyWingman, LLC published in Sep 2015.

Notes Page

CHAPTER TEN
RESPECT: BORING BURL

Never allow someone to insult you.

I have always been the naïve sort, especially when it came to girls. You want to believe what you are told, but often that is a lie. I am not disparaging anyone or any gender, because as my good friend BB King once sang, "We all lie a little."[19] But sometimes the truth may be worse than a lie, according to how it is told. The only way to spin this chapter is to come right out and say it:

Boy you're boring!!!

There, I said it. That is what my first girlfriend told me. I will not use names, so-as to protect myself versus the other person, but she told me that I was boring. I do not recall when, where, or why, I just know she said it. When it is your first love (or first lust), you tend to overlook certain things, a quality you lose as you age. I have always held to the biblical principle of being "slow to anger," and slow I was in this situation because I did not know what to say or do. So, I explained the situation to my Dad, and oh boy, did he have something to say about it!

THE INSIGHT

Before I embarked on what could become a journey—the end of a lasting relationship—I wanted to make certain I had a private conversation with Dad. Our dad avidly played solitaire. We had a fenced-in yard, and Dad would sometimes sit in the backyard and play solitaire. On that afternoon he sat engaged in a match of wits with himself and enjoying the spring breeze. I thought my approach to him was smooth, as it had always been. Being well mannered and an expert at tact, I slowly approached the conversation with a hypothetical.

Because neither of us liked small talk much, I tried the "Can I ask you about something that's been bothering me?" approach. So much for the hypothetical. In his classic Burl Randolph fashion, he responded in the affirmative without ever looking up from his card game. I explained how someone had told me that they did not understand why I never wanted to do anything they ever wanted to do, and that I never seemed to be doing anything when they called.

"Well, what did she say?" Dad asked, without ever looking up.

I replied, "She said I was boring".

Have you ever seen a car come to a screeching halt? How about a car slamming on the brakes then doing a 180-degree turn? That is really the only way I can describe Dad stopping the card game and looking up at me so quickly that it frightened me.

"What?" he said rather loudly.

"She said I'm boring."

His head reared back as he slowly sat up straight, cards clutched in his hand and said, "Man, there's no way I would be around someone who called me boring! I would never speak to her again!"

His reaction surprised me, and to make certain I had the full impact of his wrath, he topped it off with, "Don't EVER let anyone insult you!"

THE INSPIRATION

There, now everyone should know why I do not suffer fools gladly. I am truly slow to anger, but my temper has been known to go from 0 to 60 in about eight seconds! To accentuate the point about insults, a good friend while at military school, Odie Walls, made the comment once that, "People say things in jest that they really mean."

In short, people insult you by saying something as a joke. Because we often do not fully listen to what people are saying to us or how they say it, we can become the butt of many jokes or the punchline to someone's standup comedy routine. Have you ever felt that way?

Now, I am not saying that I cannot take a good joke and even laugh at myself, but sometimes the best quality of a joke is that it is grounded in some truth. Has anyone ever said something to you or about you that left you speechless? Was that person a supervisor, coworker, so-called friend, or fellow parishioner? Was it someone that you do not even know? Let's see how this may occur.

1. **Performance Counseling**. Performance counseling is NOT a time to personally attack someone, but to assess their performance. People may exhibit behavior that you do not like, and it is alright to tell them, but not for the first time in a formal counseling session. As a Battalion Commander (CEO), Company Commanders (Regional Managers) would sometime arrive early prior to assuming command. During that period, I observed behaviors either first or second hand that I did not like or approve of. This motivated me, the CEO, to create The Observation: Things I had observed that I either questioned, did not like, or did not approve of, that the person should know prior to any formal counseling session.

   The Observation served as a respectful and effective way to convey what I observed and how I felt about it. I ended The Observation with, "If the behavior in question continues, this Observation will become part of the counseling record." I do not make threats but statements of fact. I do not believe in blindsiding people or using counseling as a weapon.

2. **Coaching**. People are motivated in different ways and insults should not be one of those ways. Yes, I played sports and coaches say things to motivate players: "Can't you run any faster?" "I know you got more in the tank than that!" "Stop holding back!" All those statements seem perfectly acceptable to me because they are meant to inspire players to do better. What is not acceptable is: "I don't know how the heck you made this team." "Who told you that you could play ball?" "You play like a girl!" Because insults are personal denigrations of a person, they generally do not motivate but aggravate and create ill-will among the players.

3. **Mentoring**. Yes, I wrote it, mentoring. Mentoring dysfunction is rampant because many people do not understand mentoring. Mentoring is a voluntary developmental relationship based on mutual trust and respect that creates understanding for someone through the sharing experiences.[20] Mentoring is NOT a time for the mentor to lord their experiences over the mentee in a

manner that leaves the person feeling less equipped. It should be a common expectation that the mentor has more experience in something than the mentee. If not, why would they be the mentor?

4. **Leaders**. Being someone's boss does not provide the avenue or the right to insult them, but it occurs all the time. "Why do I always need to supervise you? Don't you know how to do anything?" Hello, that's what supervisors do. Supervise and provide guidance to help improve performance, complete a task, and accomplish the mission.

5. **Coworkers**. Being coworkers means that you work WITH not against each other. I have had peers tell me when my performance was lacking in a manner that I truly appreciated, and it made me better. I have also observed a coworker chastise another coworker about their performance. Helping each other is how the workplace becomes better not bitter.

6. **Friends**. Let's go back to the Odie Walls example: "People say things in jest (as a joke) that they really mean." Do you have a "friend" that consistently and relentlessly cracks jokes about you and only you? Does the cracking increase as the crowd gets larger? Do the cracks make you feel insulted or belittled? That is a So-Called Friend because a true friend does not find constant fault, but constant favor.

Joking around with friends is common, but not being the butt of all jokes. If this sounds like one of your friends, you may want to find a new friend.

7. **Family**. This category may be the most hurtful. It was written in The Gospel According to Matthew that, "A prophet is without honor in his own country." Sometimes those closest to you may say the meanest things. Try to forgive them as you forgive yourself because maybe we all have been guilty of that indiscretion.

The military proved very difficult for me to keep my mouth shut. I found the best way to undermine the under-miner is to outfox them.

THE APPLICATION

It was the summer of 1988. I had just completed training at Fort Sill, Oklahoma, and arrived at my first Active Duty assignment at Fort Hood Texas. The Army had instilled in me a wanderlust to see the world. While in the Army Reserves, I had traveled to Germany and had the opportunity to deploy to Nicaragua. I skipped Nicaragua though in favor of graduating from Iowa State University. Arriving at Fort Hood all bright-eyed and bushy-tailed, I never intended to apply Dad's pearl of wisdom so soon: "Don't EVER let anyone insult you!"

After meeting a few of the other African American Lieutenants, a prevailing theme occurred surrounding one Captain in particular. The theme provided a forewarning about the White Captain's attitude toward African American officers. I listened intently on how they described the officer, capturing every detail to formulate my strategy on how to engage him.

Although a First Lieutenant, as a Captain, the White officer still outranked me. I could not pick this officer from a line-up of one because I only knew his name. Ah, the beauty of nametags on uniforms! As I approached a Captain and rendered a sharp hand salute, I noticed his name. He returned the gesture and asked me, "So, what historically Black college or university (HBCU) did you graduate from?" I would have been utterly shocked and dismayed had I not received the "G2"—intelligence—about this officer.

With this as my first encounter as a new Lieutenant arriving at the unit, it could have shaped my opinion of the organization and the officer. I took the snide remark to imply that all African American officers must have attended, graduated, and were commissioned from an HBCU.

The Captain had fallen right into my trap! With such a well-planned response to the question, I casually replied, "*Iowa State University, Sir.*" Shocked and dismayed, the Captain profusely proclaimed alumni status at the same institution.

Please make note: being associated with an HBCU did not insult me. Previously, HBCUs were the only higher education institutions that African Americans could attend without fear of ridicule, bias, and downright discrimination. William Edward Burghardt (WEB) DuBois was the first African American PhD from Harvard, although he completed his undergraduate studies at Fisk University, an HBCU.[21] [22] Booker T. Washington founded the highly successful Tuskegee Normal and Industrial Institute (shortened to the Tuskegee Institute) based on his educational experiences at Hampton University, an HBCU.[23] [24] I believe that HBCUs were instrumental in and to the African American scholastic process in the 1800s.

Military men attending non-HBCUs were the precursor to both Dr. DuBois and Dr. Washington. Lieutenant Henry O. Flipper was the first African American cadet to graduate from the United States Military Academy at WestPoint in 1877. A former slave no less, Flipper graduated and served in the Army Quartermaster Corps while he could.[25] Colonel Charles Young, also a former slave, was the third African American to graduate from WestPoint in 1889.[26] Undoubtedly, you are likely wondering why I jumped over the second African American WestPoint graduate, second lieutenant John Hanks Alexander. Alexander was a renowned and respected WestPoint cadet who graduated number 32 of 64 cadets in 1887. He was assigned to the Ninth Cavalry Regiment and was purportedly the first and only African American officer in the Army commissioned to lead troops in combat. Unfortunately, Alexander died at 30 years old from apoplexy.[27] This is likely why his notoriety is limited.

By 1988, military history had long proven that African Americans could be educated outside of HBCUs. All those fine men paved the way for many African Americans to attend non-HBCUs. Without any prior knowledge of me, the White Captain provided the bias that all African American officers must be the same. With the insult given, I had devised an answer to my potential oppressor that shocked him.

African American officers routinely endure those types of events at the hands of White superior officers in the military. I experienced and heard of such ignorance throughout my military career. The fact that I had attended Iowa State appalled me even more. Iowa State University. IOWA STATE UNIVERSITY. There were not many African Americans who attended Iowa State University (ISU) when I graduated, and I had never endured such blatant in-your-face discrimination until I reached Fort Hood. I soon discovered that insults were routine in the workforce, in the Army, and in all branches of military service.

With that experience, I also discovered something about myself: I had no tolerance to be insulted. I am surprised that I survived in the Army for nearly 32 years. As Navy Captain (O6) Al Davis said at my Defense Intelligence Agency (DIA) farewell luncheon, "Burl Randolph does not suffer fools gladly." If not for CAPTAIN Davis, the only African American officer I ever had as a direct Supervisor, I would not have known that my Dad's sage advice on insults would be so on point.

It also supported Dad's assertion that it is alright to stand up for yourself. CAPTAIN Davis' temperament is what I recall the most about him. We spoke candidly about the stereotype of the Angry Black Man and how it could derail a career. Although I have been known to raise my voice, my experiences with insults are what contributes to my Recovering Perfectionism.[28] Dealing with insults also helped me pursue humility and civility over arrogance and insolence.

Presenting for the QC Economic Empowerment Network. Left, Lunchtime Learning June 2016. Right, QC Black Expo Feb 2018.

Notes Page

CHAPTER ELEVEN
PRIDE: DRESS THE PART

When people see you, make them think twice.

I have always been a large man. Not "Big and Tall" large, but 5x5 large—five-foot-tall and five foot wide. Okay, I have never been five-foot-wide, but I sure felt like it. And I am five foot eight inches tall. It would be convenient to say that I come from a "large" family, but no one stuffed Twinkies and Ho-Ho's down my throat. The beauty in writing a narrative is that the people who know you can verify what you write ... or not. All I know is that I became tired of being defined by the size of my body versus my brain.

Coach William Burgett was a lovable man. I believe he liked me because my name best described his appearance: burly. Coach Burgett had a deep and thunderous voice and when he spoke, everyone heard him. On this day, me and Willie Davis forgot the tee shirt portion of our gym suits when Coach Burgett announced, "Willie don't need no tee shirt. Give Big Burl a tee shirt."

Willie thought that was funnier than a Bugs Bunny cartoon, and I heard about it for the remainder of the school year—an entire semester. Willie had an uncanny imitation of Coach Burgett, so I cringed every time I heard it. Soon, the entire eighth grade class of Martin Luther King, Jr., Junior High School repeated the phrase whenever they saw me. Although I knew that this was not said to denigrate me, after a while it became monotonous to hear. I knew that kids always wanted to have fun but geez, why was it at my expense?

THE INSIGHT

Those of us who are large but lovable can understand my pain. I knew that I would be attending Paseo Senior High School and my intel sources indicated that Willie would not. 'Yes! I thought, no more **Big Burl** comments!' I forgot that only Willie would be attending a different high school. To my dismay, everyone else from our eighth-grade class attended high school with me. Once I joined the football team, the Big Burl nickname resurfaced. To assuage my new moniker, I decided to approach it a little differently in high school.

I wrote BBB on all my documents. Notebooks, papers, locker, gym clothes, everything. After a couple of weeks, people began to ask, 'What does BBB stand for?' I always replied the same:

"Big Bad Burl"

I thought, "If I'm going to have a nickname I do not want, I will use it to my advantage." It became sort of catchy, with people saying, "Hey BBB."

Oddly enough years later, I would become an avid B.B. King fan, learning that his real name was Riley B. King. The B.B stood for Blues Boy, his road name on the Chitlin Circuit. The Chitlin Circuit was the African American Entertainer's version of "The Green Door," the venues throughout the Southern U.S. where African American musical entertainers could perform. Although this is fascinating, I digress and return to my story.

THE INSPIRATION

As a senior, BBB became B^3 (pronounced B-cubed) at the urging of one of my calculus or algebra cohorts. Unfortunately, bigness continued to characterize my junior year. I began to take notice however, of something significant: my Dad dressed impeccably. Even as a hi-lift operator, Dad wore a pressed uniform at the beginning of each week, and he looked sharp and crisp. At home, Dad might wear work clothes when in his garden or puttering around the house. During the weekends however, Dad dressed sharply.

In the summer he normally wore tailored short sleeve shirts, nice slacks, dress shoes, and his trademark brimmed hat that matched his outfits. I learned later that those hats where purchased at Michael's Fine Clothing of Kansas City and cost $25 a pop, even in the 1970s!

I thought, "Maybe I should only wear dress clothes to school, so I would not feel so fat?" I noticed that all the large male entertainers were well dressed: Barry White, Luther Vandross, Fats Domino, Chubby Checker, and B.B King. Of course, they all had the distinct advantage that I did not: They could sing.

I believe Dad knew of my self-consciousness, because when I asked him why he always dressed up he replied: "When you *know* you look good on the outside, it makes you feel good on the inside."

To some that may seem shallow, but I invite you to walk a mile in my sized 10.5 EEEE shoes. Or perhaps you could try on a pair of my "husky" jeans?

Dressing up daily provided for me something that even JROTC did not give me: Pride. Although I lost a significant amount of weight during the summer between my junior and senior school years, I gained my pride by dressing the part. Because I had conditioned the entire school to only see me dressed up, anything other than that caused a stir. As a senior, I had been working a part-time job for four years. I had a car. And when others were buying Members Only jackets, I bought a leather coat! I was styling!

Having pride in yourself is critical as a leader. No, I do not mean arrogance, but pride: self-respect, dignity, and self-esteem. People who might otherwise be good leaders fail because they lack self-esteem. Would you follow a leader that did not exhibit self-esteem? Based on the infantry motto, "Follow Me," would you expect people to follow you if you never gave them a reason to? There are several considerations to make when establishing whether you have pride:

1. How do you feel about yourself?
2. How much does it matter what others think?
3. Are you comfortable being labeled a Boring Burl or dubbing yourself BBB?
4. What can you do to change your perspective of yourself?
5. Do you have justifiable esteem in your accomplishments?

These questions may seem mundane to you, and I am happy for you. But to the person striving to be a leader but has challenges that must be overcome, the ability to answer and overcome these questions is vital. Even more vital is how these potential solutions may be applied.

THE APPLICATION

Even as I write this, I am the largest I have been in over 20 years. I struggled with my weight throughout my years in the Army. Although I lost weight and maintained it for a while, something would happen that deterred my diet—an injury sustained during physical training. I did, however, maintain my pride. There were likely several turning points for me in my battle with the bulge, but one I choose to recount: First Sergeant Harold Lewis.

Our new First Sergeant (1SG) made it plain and clear that being overweight was unacceptable. Since we had just returned from a National Training Center (NTC) rotation, 1SG Lewis bid us a good vacation. We would need it when we returned. Although on profile—a rest period from physical training (PT) based on a medically verified injury— I knew 1SG Lewis did not joke about PT. Bravo Battery, 3rd of the 82nd Field Artillery was trimming the fat!

If you could walk, run, or hobble, your butt conducted PT. 1SG Lewis ran the Bravo Battery two, then three, then four miles a day, three to four days a week. This occurred after his weightlifting session before he came to work. I had never encountered anyone in my life that had done so much PT or had such passion about it. First Sergeant served in Vietnam and provided me a great honor to serve with him, no matter how tough it was on the body!

Because of my profile, and I felt out of shape, "dressing the part" seemed difficult. No matter how starched my uniform looked, I did not feel like a Soldier. During one of our formations, one of the Assistant Section Chiefs, a Staff Sergeant (E-6), just laughed at all the complaining and said, "It don't matter. First Sergeant has always been this way!"

After formation I asked him what he meant by that. "Sir," he said, "1SG Lewis was my Drill Sergeant [the noncommissioned officer cadre that transforms civilians into military personnel] when I was a Private and he was a Staff Sergeant."

"So what?" I replied.

"Sir, First Sergeant used to weigh 240 pounds and did the EXACT same things then, he does NOW! IT DON'T MATTER!"

I verified these facts with 1SG Lewis, who told me that no Soldier of his would ever be ostracized by and from the Army for being overweight. He vowed to do everything in his power to make certain that did not happen. First Sergeant inspired me to change my attitude and I knew what I had to do.

Although I had been losing weight and mildly exercising, it was not enough to regain pride in myself. I ramped up the diet and exercise volume between April and June of that year and set my goal on the Battery Four Mile Run, scheduled for a sweltering afternoon at Fort Hood, Texas, our duty station. Decked out in our Battery PT uniform, I came out last and fell into formation in front of my platoon (a section of 30-50 personnel normally led by a second lieutenant). Because we were waiting on the Battery Commander and a few other things, 1SG Lewis asked me to step out of the formation for a sidebar.

We always had great rapport, so he was direct, but gentle when he said, "Sir, you don't have to do this." He went on to tell me that, "You are NOT cleared for PT, let alone a four-mile run. We all know you have a real injury. You don't have to do this."

Although I truly appreciated his concern and told him so, I replied, "First Sergeant, yes, I do have to do this because I am the leader."

He told me, "Okay." Then the Battery Commander arrived, and we took off. I completed the run without falling out because no one ever fell out of 1SG Lewis' formations. If they did, we just turned around and got them, no matter how many times they fell out. We started and finished together.

This was not the first time my service to country was on the line. Several years earlier a rappelling accident at Fort Riley, Kansas, Advanced Camp threatened to derail my commissioning as an Army officer because of a twisted right knee. I was required to participate in a four-mile company run as the pace man—fourth squad leader—or be medically discharged. With a weekend of aspirin and ice packs, I made the run that Monday morning when others did not. Suffering from a stress fracture years later while on

Active Duty, I was again threatened with discharge but conducted and passed my PT test. This time, however, it felt different. It was not a matter of survival, but a matter of pride.

After completing that run and all the others, I felt much more pride in wearing my uniforms, no matter which uniform it was. As I continued to struggle with my weight, I would fight the good fight, diet, exercise, and buy new clothes as necessary. I learned throughout the years that what others thought of me was not as important as what I thought of myself. I also took my duties as a leader much more seriously. Because no one ever asked me to lead them, I applied for the job. I had an obligation to live up to the standard. Even today, I still dress the part to maintain my self-respect.

First Lieutenant Randolph leading Bravo Battery, 3rd Battalion, 82nd Field Artillery in parade practice for 1st Cavalry Division, Fort Hood, Texas, June 1989.

Notes Page

PHOTOGRAPHS

(L) BenElla Randolph (R) Burl Randolph pinning Second Lieutenant Burl Randolph, Jr., Kemper Military School and College, May 1983.

Commissioning Class, 1983, Kemper Military
School and College.

Promotion to Captain Sep 1, 1990 by the 3rd of the 82nd Field Artillery Battalion Commander and spouse Terry Randolph. This was after alert for deployment to Saudi Arabia for Operation Desert Shield.

Captain Randolph in front of the S2 548 tracked vehicle during Operation Desert Shield. Kingdom of Saudi Arabia, December 1990. My first assignment as an intelligence officer was in combat.

Promotion to Major at the Defense Intelligence Agency,
August 1998. Promotion party from L to R: Terry Randolph,
me, Colonel Harry G. Simmeth, Jr., and Captain Josh Jones.

Terry and me.

The Family
who
attended the
ceremony.

Me at Red Square, Moscow, Russia, June 2001.

LTC promotion somewhere in Iraq, Operation Iraqi Freedom One, March 1, 2003. Pinned by Colonel Robert B. Smith, USAF and my first words a newly promoted LTC.

First LTC Command: Votkinsk Portal Monitoring Facility, Votkinsk, Russia. October 2003. Defense Threat Reduction Agency.

Command (CEO) photos, June 2004, Baltimore Recruiting Battalion. CSM Donald Hall in the background.

My final event at the Orioles baseball game with General Richard Cody, Army Vice Chief of Staff, Ace of Cakes Chef, and Orioles officials.

Promotion to Colonel in Iraq, April 2008 by then LTG Lloyd Austin, Multi-National Corps Commanding General.

Terry, Dominic, Derek, and CSM Randy Bailey, watching the promotion from Fort Meade, Maryland.

Flying over
Iraq, June 2008.

Return from
Operation
Iraqi Freedom
07-09, March
2009.

US Army War College. Left photo: Veterans Day speech at
Carlisle Middle School, Nov 2009. Right photo: Waiting to
steal a base during softball. On base means I got a hit!

Commanding troops at Fort Sam Houston, Texas, July 2012.

Deputy Chief of Staff for Intelligence and Security, G2, US Army Sustainment Command, Rock Island Arsenal, Rock Island, Illinois, July 2013.

Retirement Ceremony, April 24, 2014, Rock Island Arsenal

Family with the retirement Official Party

Graduation from the University of Phoenix at the Chicagoland
Campus, June 2018 with the Doctor of Management in
Organizational Leadership. I was conferred in January 2018.

CHAPTER TWELVE
RESPONSIBILITY: OWN IT

Define your own success.

Even in the best relationships, unexpected conversations occur. Out of all the conversations with my Dad, this one had to be the most liberating. Every man seeks to make his father proud, and I believe that every *good* father wants more for his children. My father was no exception and ensured each of us had the opportunity to attend college if we so desired. As I mentioned before, we were a single income family, but Dad saved ferociously. I wrote "ferocious" because to provide the opportunity for seven children to attend college required fierce discipline. Saving money and college were not the topic of this unexpected conversation.

THE INSIGHT

As I write this and recall this event, I now understand the apprehension my sons have when I come to their bedrooms to chat with them. Normally when a parent goes to a child's bedroom, the child believes that trouble is on the horizon, or right now! I was not in trouble. My Dad just wanted to know my plans. *"I want to be like you,"* I replied, not trying to suck up. Then I heard something that no man expects to hear, but probably needs to: "Don't focus on being like me and making my mistakes. Make your own mistakes."

I thought the pearls of wisdom ended there, but then came the critical phrase:

"Be your own man."

Yes, I was stunned. I would challenge any man to recall hearing these words from his father as a freshman in high school or any other time. Apparently, I am not the brightest bulb in the lamp, and I needed further clarification. Dad sensed my confusion and said, "What may have been a mistake for me may not be a mistake for you. That's why you need to be your own man and find your own way."

I believe we began the conversation about the future, the importance of education, and that it should at least be a consideration. As effortlessly as he had come into my room, Dad departed. As I stood there with my mouth gapped open, I could not fully grasp or appreciate the gift I had just received.

THE INSPIRATION

This was heavy conversation for a 14-year-old boy. I now had the opportunity to do what I wanted, be who I wanted, and pursue what I wanted, but what were all of those? As the years passed by, my druthers continuously changed from firefighter-paramedic, to wealthy businessman, to world-renowned writer, to high school dropout to Soldier. Throughout that entire period, I always had a desire to serve and to help other people. Even then, I knew:

- I knew how to get what I wanted.
- I did not take advantage of people.
- Losing my parents was my greatest fear.

As the years progressed, I also learned that:

- I do not always *need* what I want.
- People will try to take advantage of you if you let them.
- Losing my parents remained my greatest fear but would not stop me from living my life.

All those epiphanies would lead me down both good and bad paths throughout the remainder of my life. Some values would be harder to maintain than others, but I committed to them as best I could.

1. **Always treat people fairly**. Being a Soldier most of my life you might think that I enjoyed the cookie-cutter, assembly line, everything-is-the-same approach, and you would be wrong. Treating everyone the same is not only

impossible, it is insulting because we are born as individuals. You cannot treat everyone the same, but you can treat everyone fairly. Fairness is what people really want—equity, individuality, and respect.

2. **Know the difference between the have-to and the want-to.** I normally received punishment because I failed to complete the requirement, the have-to, in favor of pursuing my desires, the want-to. This shortfall was not a youthful indiscretion but is why I and most people get in trouble today: failure to do what is required. Although I knew this, what can you expect from a 14-year old?

3. **Respect given is not always respect received but give it anyway.** People may disrespect you, attempt to take advantage of you, and take your kindness for weakness however, you cannot change other people. On how to deal with disrespect, please refer to Chapter Ten: Boring Burl. Regarding taking advantage of you—let people *think* they are smarter than you, until they discover they are not. Never let them see you sweat—your kindness will render their ugliness moot.

4. **Never pick a fight, but if you must fight, win.** Some people are natural fighters, but I do not consider myself in that group. I do not look for or randomly pursue fights. When I get wound up, however, I fight to win. As a Soldier,

fighting became even more appalling because an insult can lead to a fight can lead to an international incident, and then to war. I keep my friends close and my enemies closer, but I have less enemies than friends (I think!).

5. **Focus on making my parents proud.** Death is currently undefeated amongst us mere mortals, so I decided not to focus on something I could not beat or change. Living my life so that I would make my parents proud, keep the RANDOLPH name untarnished, and establish a legacy to pass on allowed me to move on from my fears. I once heard a wise man say, "It is not the years in your life but the life in your years that define a quality life."[29]

Although those were childish thoughts, they would carry me throughout my life. Those thoughts or values would also lead me to decide on a vocation that my family would have a love/hate relationship with: Becoming a Soldier.

THE APPLICATION

The application of being my own man was not an easy one. It would be that piece of advice that began my mentorship journey. Although the decision to become a Soldier was an easy one, the road was not. When I was growing up, westerns, war movies, and war television series were quite popular. There was no internet or social media to gather information from. You either saw it on television, read about it in the newspaper, learned about it in history class, or researched the topic in an encyclopedia. Because I had access to all four means, becoming a Soldier was a fantasy that became a reality from an early age.

I recall that in the fourth grade we were required to create an individual project. While most of the other boys were designing rocket ships and race cars, I built a fort. Yes, you read correctly, a fort—a fortification that housed land-based Army personnel and their families and from which Soldiers deployed. I used every popsicle stick, piece of green and brown construction paper, and stick figures I could get my hands on in the classroom to build my fort. True to form, the other kids laughed at me, attacked the fort, and laid siege upon my project, but I prevailed until … I got sick! When I returned to school from my illness, the fort had effectively been overrun. No amount of popsicle sticks, glue, or brown paper could save it. My first military defeat!

Fast forward to high school, where I joined the JROTC under the leadership of MSG Scott, my first military mentor. I am uncertain what MSG Scott saw in a fat, shy kid from the hood, but he taught me that I was a fighter, I could do whatever I set my mind too, and that I had a winning spirit. He also brought out in me the desire to serve. Because of MSG Scott, Sergeant Major (SGM) John W. Quinn, and JROTC, I learned the military histories of my father and uncles, and I hopefully inspired my sons and some of my nephews to serve. Besides rising through the ranks from cadet private to cadet colonel, I also earned several Army ROTC scholarships to various colleges and was nominated to the United States Military and Naval Academies. I will explain this further in Chapter Fourteen, Education.

I met my other mentors in JROTC, such as Lieutenant Colonel (LTC) Nathaniel Field, the Director of Army Instruction (DAI) for the Kansas City, Missouri school district, and then Captain (CPT) Harry Simmeth, the Chief Inspector for the Annual General Inspection. LTC Field lobbied for me to become an Army officer, and CPT Simmeth provided me his business card and told me: "If you ever need anything from me, my parents know how to contact me." I took him up on his offer over the years as we kept in touch and crossed paths while on active duty.

At Kemper Military School, LTC John Parker, the Professor of Military Science (PMS) kept me focused and motivated when I incurred what I thought was a career-ending injury. He ensured that I met the requirements for graduation and commissioning. LTC James 'Jim' Taylor was the Unit Administrator (a high-level civilian position) for the Reserve unit I volunteered to serve in while at Iowa State University. When I completed the -1 or list of accomplishments for my first officer evaluation report (OER), he looked it over and told me it was a no-go because it did not have anything important on it. When I told him that my boss knew what I had accomplished, he replied that was incorrect and said, "Man, you need to learn how to toot your own horn. You're the only one who knows the tune." That advice served me well over the years.

LTC Armstrong was my first active duty mentor and taught me in a very short period, what it meant to be an officer at the tactical and operational levels. He explained that I needed to be better, faster, and stronger than my competition, if I expected to make the Army a career. Although that sounded like a promo for the TV show The Six Million Dollar Man, LTC Armstrong said it, and it was true.

I selected this short list of mentors because they helped me in my formative years in pursuing my path of becoming my own man in the Army. Although Dad provided the wisdom, he also gave me the responsibility to act on it. Whether in the military, civilian life, or whatever it is I do, I own it because being your own person requires you to take responsibility for yourself. With that said, I still had a long way to go after Dad liberated me.

CHAPTER THIRTEEN
OBEDIENCE: STRANDED

"A hard head makes a soft behind." Burl Randolph

Dad was not a man prone to anger, but when he got mad, watch out! The rules were simple in our home. As with most people, however, I resisted following the rules. "Following the rules" meant being "obedient." My philosophy is that rules are not made to be broken, but to keep us safe (normally from ourselves) and to level the playing field. The Ten Commandments are not the Ten Suggestions, ignorance of the law is no excuse, and defying the rules of Burl Randolph had consequences.

Once again, a nice, sunny day and a girl were involved. Trouble seemed to follow me when I followed that girl, but I digress.

THE INSIGHT

I only needed to follow one set of directions: "Stop driving that car until it gets fixed." I could only drive back and forth to high school. I do not recall what car repair I needed, but I only had a limited range to drive it. Not only did I overshoot my range but played hooky from school doing it!

How it started, where it started, and why it started are not important. What is important was that I was not in school, my car broke down traveling to the park (I think) and I became stranded as my passengers bailed on me! So much for friendship. As I looked in my rearview mirror, hazard lights flashing, and who did I see driving up behind me? My Dad! The story gets even murkier here because I do not recall if my passengers bailed before or after Dad passed the car, all I know is that Dad apparently did not notice the car.

So, as I sat there stranded, with no AAA towing service, USAA auto insurance, cellphone (not invented yet), or gas station in sight, my thoughts were consumed with, *How I would get out of this mess?* And, *what would my parents say?* Based on the route my Dad took, I surmised that he might be visiting Aunt Virginia, his sister. This gave me at least an hour or two to devise a plan to get out of this chaos! I needed to get the car at least near a street facing home along my school route, avoid getting caught ditching school, and find a way to get help. The two hours seemed like forever!

I sat patiently waiting to see Dad's car returning from the opposite direction. When I did, I honked and honked and honked my horn with one hand and waved out the window with the other. He kept right on driving, so I figured, *oh well, guess I'll have to walk home.* As I closed the car hood, I saw his 1975 maroon Chevy Belair pull up behind me. Dad got out of the car with a scowl on his face and said, "Open the hood." I popped the hood and lifted it up. Dad looked underneath the hood, then looked at me and said,

"A hard head makes a soft behind."

He told me to close everything up and motioned for me to get in his car. When we got home, mom happily greeted us, but wondered why we were together. When I told her about the car, she already knew that I had skipped school. Mom simply said, "What did your father say?" Because he went back to their bedroom, I told her exactly what he said and asked what it meant. She said, "You're lucky he didn't knock your head off. He told you to stop driving that car."

I do not recall much except that I did not have much money that summer because it all went to pay for the tow truck and car repairs. That incident inspired me to do better.

THE INSPIRATION

Although I had gotten better with being obedient, hardheadedness followed me throughout college, and even as an active duty Army officer. Even with the requirements for standards, discipline, and following orders, I still had a bit of an obstinate streak in me. There are times when it may be alright to have that streak when innovation or safety is concerned, but not for personal gain. The biblical perspective from I Samuel, Chapter 15, verse 2 is very piercing to my spirit as a leader: To obey is better than sacrifice. Please ponder that perspective for a minute.

As military professionals, we often speak about the great sacrifices we make to serve our country. The question now is: Are we serving in earnest by obeying? What is the price of our obstinance, contriteness, or disobedience? Obedience is a great combat multiplier because:

1. **Obedience builds teams**. Some may have you believe that obedience is divisive, but only to those who wish to sow the seeds of discord. The essence of collaboration is everyone being obedient to the agreed upon group norms.

2. **Obedience builds confidence**. When you follow directions and are rewarded by success, obedience builds your confidence in the person, process, or premise that you were obedient too.

3. **Obedience builds trust**. Certain qualities are necessary to gain trust: integrity, sincerity, dependability, and obedience.

4. **Obedience may dictate life or death**. On a chaotic battlefield, obedience to orders, tactics, techniques, and

procedures (TTP), may be the difference between life and death.

Disobedience causes disarray, undermines authority, and fractures organizations. I also believe leaders have an obligation to ask questions to ensure that orders are clear. As a COO, I once told one of my CEOs, "As an officer I have the right to disagree, but not disobey. So, it's my duty to voice my concerns." Blind obedience never sees straight and can get you into trouble. Reckless disobedience may have an even higher price.

THE APPLICATION

Although I am a staunch disciplinarian, sometimes it takes hearing a different perspective to truly appreciate the gravity of a value. By 2006, the United States had been at war with Iraq for six years. During that time, I had deployed on Operation Iraqi Freedom I, continued deployments to Russia enforcing the Strategic Arms Reduction Treaty (START), completed two successful years of Battalion Command (CEO), and began a third year. With just shy of 19 years on active duty, I truly believed I knew what enforcing standards meant. That is, until I met CSM Randy Bailey.

I had already begun my third year of Battalion Command, and CSM Randy Bailey would be my third Command Sergeant Major. CSM Bailey told me at the conclusion of our first meeting, "Sir, we will be friends for life." I thought no truer words were spoken, until I heard a later statement he made. CSM Bailey had a knack for many proverbs that I treasure and carry with me throughout life. Most of the adages were positive, upbeat, inspiring, and meant to build up not tear down. He meant for his statement on obedience to have shock and awe, and it did.

We had gathered our Company Leadership Teams or CLTs which consisted of the Company Commander and the First Sergeant (Regional Manager and Assistant Regional Manager) for a meeting. CSM Bailey spoke about standards, discipline, and absolute obedience to legal orders. His passionate, fired up, and sincere statement went something like this:

> *Ladies and Gentlemen, this is not a game. Our country is at war. We need you to absolutely follow the orders of the Battalion Commander because when you leave here, many of you will deploy. The failure of a Soldier at any rank to follow orders in this day and age may cost them their life, or the lives of the Soldiers around them.*

We were an Army Recruiting Battalion, so those were intense words. I asked CSM Bailey afterward what inspired him to say that and he replied, "You did, Sir."

"Me? What did I have to do with it?" I asked.

CSM Bailey reminded me of the conversation we had when I told him that I was extra tough on the Company Commanders because they all deployed directly after leaving our unit.

"Wingman," he said, "I cannot be any less intense on those First Sergeants because they will likely never deploy as 79 Romeo's [permanent Recruiters]."

As each of these young men and women changed command, those that had never deployed received the opportunity. Little did I know the opportunity had grown beyond Captains. As my time ended in Battalion Command, I learned why "friends are better than money."

In mid-2007 I received a call from Military Intelligence branch from one of my former Company Commanders. He called to warn me that the combat zone required intense leadership, so former Battalion Commanders, fresh out of command, were being deployed. I thanked him and because I wanted out of recruiting, I had two choices: Iraq heavy or Iraq light. This meant deployment with a unit or as an individual augmentee. I chose the unit.

I deployed with the XVIII Airborne Corps to Iraq on the last 15-month rotation for the Army. This was my first and only assignment in the airborne world. I met and served with some of the finest people I know, from all branches of service, coalition forces, government civilians and contractors. It was also where I met and served with a great leader and mentor, then, LTG Lloyd

Austin. The words from my Dad rang in my ears. The message from CSM Bailey became a reality. My own words about deployment had come to fruition for me. It made me truly appreciate the importance of obedience and learned about the sacrifices obedience sometimes required.

The training for this deployment caused a separation of our family for the first time. I moved to Fort Bragg, North Carolina in August 2007. I skyped with my family nightly during the separation until February 2008. Yes, I returned for holidays, birthdays, and Derek's baptism (January 2008) during that period, but spent most of my time preparing for combat. My obedience to my oath of office for the defense of our nation required a sacrifice I had not previously known. Although obedience may be better than sacrifice, it certainly does feel like sacrifice when you are executing your responsibilities.

The final year in command, 2007. Change of Command below with CSM Randy Bailey.

Notes Page

CHAPTER FOURTEEN
EDUCATION: *"I'M DROPPING OUT"*

No one can take away your education.

Manhood is weird. Men have the bizarre notion that we must always prove ourselves in ways that can be detrimental. "Map? I don't need no stinkin map! I know where I'm going!" (as the family ends up halfway to Des Moines while searching for Worlds of Fun amusement park in Kansas City). "You need instructions? I've never used instructions to build anything in my life!" (which explains the lack of furniture, complex kids' toys, and small appliances). "I don't need school. I'm dropping out!" There is no snappy retort for this one. Dropping out of high school is injurious to a person's future.

Dropping out of high school is so injurious that the military does not accept high school dropouts because they normally do not complete basic training.[30] There is a direct correlation between aptitudes (measured by the Armed Forces Qualification Test – AFQT) and high school diploma recipients, because most recruits who have both qualifications do not drop out.[31]   To the contrary, those who dropped out of high school and later passed the General Education Development (GED) examination that made them eligible for Army enlistment, graduated basic training at a higher rate.[32]

When I uttered the phrase 'dropping out' to my mother, needless to say (but I will say it anyway), I got an earful! I will not recount what she said, although there were no expletives. Mom was mad, furious, and just did not understand why someone at the top of his class with a bright future ahead of him would consider dropping out. That was one of those, "You need to go tell your father that you're dropping out and see what he says," conversations. I reluctantly did as I was instructed but not as quickly as Mom wanted. I waited a couple of months until the weather warmed up before approaching Dad.

THE INSIGHT

It was February in the second semester of my junior year (1980) in high school when I mentioned dropping out to my mom. I like to think that I'm no fool and pondered what she had told me. This pushed having the discussion with Dad about dropping out until April or May. Again, he was in the backyard playing a game of solitaire and enjoying the solitude that retired life can bring when I approached him.

After I went into the backyard, Dad and I had some idle chitchat and I mentioned that I had discussed something with mom. I said, "I'm thinking about dropping out of high school."

Without stopping his card game or even looking up, Dad replied, "Where you gonna live?"

Perplexed I replied, "Right here."

What came next I refer to as The Randolph Wrath, when Dad said, "Oh no you're not. You'll not drop out of high school and live here!"

The Wrath did not end there, as Dad looked me straight in my eyes, which meant I had interrupted his card game. "Why would you want to drop out of school?" he said, and Dad did not ask rhetorical questions.

"Well, I just don't see what I need it for," I said.

At this point you are all likely wondering why I felt that way, and honestly, I do not know. I held many accomplishments: top of my academic class, the JROTC Battalion Commander (CEO) as a high school junior, an unheard-of feat in those days and even now. I seemed to be well-liked and well-regarded in high school. So, what urged me to want to drop out? I didn't see the need for it. Dad surely showed me *the need* for it!

THE INSPIRATION

Out of every conversation I had with my dad, this one truly changed my life from an educational perspective. Dad had provided us kids the opportunity that he did not have: a college education. A firm foundation, values, respect for others, and education may have been the four pillars our parents instilled in us. I do not know why my older siblings did not attend college, but they all went to work, had good jobs, and constantly looked for ways to better themselves. Because those four had already moved out of the house and provided me a good example of what to do, you figure that I might have had a different mindset. Not so.

As the conversation continued, Dad provided a very passionate and pivotal answer to my response. "Man," he said, "you can't get a job on a trash truck without a high school diploma!"

I looked at him in condescending amazement and said, "A trash truck? Why do I need a high school diploma to be a garbage man?"

"Okay," said dad. "Then how does the process work?"
I said, "You grab the bags and throw them on the truck."
"Then what?" he said.
"What?" I asked.

"Once you throw the trash on the truck, then what?" Dad asked.

"The truck compresses the trash," I said.

"How?" Dad asked.

It took years before I realized that Dad used a logic train to interrogate me.

I answered Dad's question the only way I knew how with, "I don't know," looking down as I said it.

"Exactly," he said, "you don't know. And you may not learn how it works without an education." Dad went on to say, "Suit yourself, but you have my answer."

I enjoyed having a place to eat, sleep, and call home, so I continued in high school. But the conversation also made me think:

1. **What do I really know?** I was serious, I did not know what I really knew. At the time, I was focused on architecture and the military, but had very little knowledge of either. *What do you really know?*

2. **What value does my current knowledge have?** I did not have a diploma, degree, or even a certification in anything. I had only worked one job at a grocery store. With that, what value did my knowledge have? *What value does your knowledge have?*

3. **How far can I go with what I know now?** Number two answered this for me—not very far. *How far can you go with the knowledge you have now?*

4. **How far can I go with or without an education?** With an education, I could attend college, become a commissioned officer, and have something that could never be taken away from me. Without an education, I could not attend college or even join the military at any level, and possibly not even obtain a job. *How far can an education take you?*

The choice became clear: I needed to continue in school and do the best that I could. My future depended on it. Little did I know however, that my "dropout" antics would have consequences when I decided to attend college.

THE APPLICATION

Once I decided to stay in school, I continued to do the best I could and graduated 13th out of a class of 240. Not too shabby for someone who wanted to drop out a year earlier. During this time, Master Sergeant (MSG) John H. Scott, my military mentor, influenced my decision to attend college. MSG Scott asked me what my plans were after high school.

"I plan to enlist in the Army, take advantage of the accelerated promotion to E-4 based on my JROTC service, and earn promotion to sergeant. After promotion to sergeant, I would compete to be a drill sergeant for the rest of my career."

MSG Scott had a different perspective and asked me if I would consider becoming a commissioned officer? I asked with my normal 'why' response. His answer gave me pause.

"Enlisted execute policy but officers make it. From what I have seen from you I believe that you would make pretty good policies for everyone."

I remained resistant to the idea because that meant I would need to attend college. MSG Scott affirmed my suspicions and he asked me to consider the United States Military Academy (USMA) at WestPoint, New York.

Although I had decided to attend college, I had also discovered girls and had a girlfriend. Dad placed a condition on my college attendance: "You're gonna have to get straight A's if I'm paying for you to go to college," he said.

It was the one and only time I ever laughed in my Dad's face but not the last time that involuntary action got me into trouble. I said, "Dad, that's not gonna happen because I don't make straight A's now!"

Dad had a simple solution of, "Then you're gonna have to help pay for it," he said. In today's language that would be referred to as having "skin in the game."

I began researching the types of schools I wanted to attend, and where I might be able to receive scholarships. I applied to and was accepted at New Mexico Military Institute (NMMI) in Roswell, New Mexico; Wentworth Military Academy in Lexington, Missouri; and Kemper Military School and College in Boonville, Missouri. All those schools offered me partial scholarships but not enough money to sway Dad. I had to bring out the big guns. So, with MSG Scott's urging, I applied to WestPoint and I recall the fat Army Captain they sent to interview me.

The buttons on his Class A uniform were begging for mercy and his appearance infuriated MSG Scott. I did learn one thing from the interview though: the meaning of being "well-rounded." I always joked that the Captain was well-rounded based on his girth, but when he explained my activities only involved JROTC activities and that I had no depth, I understood. As my senior year began in September 1980, I decided to make up for it.

I ran for Student Council President and lost but was elected the Sergeant at Arms. I was the President of the Black Children's Club (Black History Club) and played on the high school football team as a senior. I guess I should clarify. I was *on* the team.

Because I had not played the two previous seasons, playing time was relative and limited. All those activities must have meant something because US Representative Richard Bolling provided me the required Congressional nominations for both the United States Military Academy (USMA) and United States Naval Academy (USNA).

I did not receive an appointment to attend either WestPoint or the Naval Academy because as I mentioned earlier, I was not well-rounded enough to be truly competitive. Also, regarding the Naval Academy, I could not swim, and it did not interest me. I probably should have learned, but I did not. Learning to swim is on my Bucket List.

I also applied for two- and four-year Army ROTC scholarships. Consequently, because of MSG Scott I earned a substantial scholarship to Kemper Military School and College (KMS). I truly became cognizant for the first time of what a mentor could do for you. MSG Scott completed the scholarship application and recommended me because he saw my potential and knew I needed help fulfilling it.

I continued to compete for other scholarships. This required me to attend, compete, and complete Cadet Basic Training at Fort Knox, Kentucky. After I returned, I was notified that I had earned a Two-Year TRADOC Dedicated Army ROTC

Scholarship to KMS. TRADOC stands for Training and Doctrine Command. I accepted the scholarships to Kemper and the two-year Army ROTC scholarship because those seemed like the best fit for me and Kemper was only two hours from home.

Although I had a rocky start educationally, I managed to do well for myself. I graduated from Kemper with an Associate of Arts and commissioned an Army second lieutenant. After leaving Kemper, I attended and graduated from Iowa State University with a Bachelor of Science in General Business and was selected for Active Duty. While on Active Duty, I did not attend many of the voluntary courses the Army provided because I could never be spared from my organization, or so I was always told. This increased my fondness for self-development.

Prior to selection for the rank of Major, I decided to attend Troy State University (now Troy University) and entered the Master of Business Administration (MBA) program. I also signed up for the Distance Learning Command and General Staff College (CGSC) course (now referred to as Intermediate Leader Education (ILE)). This occurred after I was not selected for the resident CGSC course at Fort Leavenworth, Kansas.

Although I worked fulltime at the Defense Intelligence Agency (DIA) while working on my MBA and CGSC, the job did not challenge me. I decided to obtain the MBA in preparation for my next assignment as a Battalion Executive Officer (Chief Operating Officer (COO)). I graduated from Troy State University with an MBA and off I went to Beckley Recruiting Battalion in Beckley, West Virginia. Unfortunately, the job of COO challenged me more than my DIA assignment, and I had only completed six months of the CGSC course.

Distance learning participants are allowed up to 24 months to complete the course, and with my duties in Beckley, I used 17 of the remaining 18 months. I finally took an academic breather with both courses of study behind me. You do not appreciate education while you are taking classes, but if you can use what you have learned to help make others successful-through mentoring, the pain and agony is all worth it.

After completing my second Lieutenant Colonel CEO position, I was selected to attend the US Army War College at Carlisle Barracks in Carlisle, Pennsylvania. The grueling pace was at a strategic, executive, and collaborative level. We were divided into seminars of about 18 students, and I served as the Seminar Chair for Seminar 18. My duties included accountability of my classmates, leading classroom discussions as appropriate, and helping classmates academically. This position consisted of ensuring classmates were postured to successfully complete the thesis writing process, ensuring we were always at the proper place at the proper time, and developing strategies to read and discuss the 50–75-page nightly reading assignments. That created the grueling part, but it helped us bond into a cohesive team.

The War College required well-roundedness and collaboration among the students, and we played sports to help build the camaraderie. We played softball in the fall, volleyball in the winter, basketball in the spring, and held a competition in late spring referred to as Jim Thorpe Days. Oddly, I became the announcer that introduced the volleyball games and decided to mimic announcer Michael Buffer and his "Let's get ready to rumble." After I did that for the first match, it became a requirement for the remaining matches. Now you know my War College claim to fame.

I often reminisce about my War College experience because the Army cliché is true: it was the best 12 months of my career. I also participated in the Eisenhower College Speaking Program (ECSP), which consisted of a team of 10–12 students visiting colleges and universities around the country to speak on national security topics. My areas of interest were military intelligence and recruiting for the All-Volunteer Force. Because this program is named after Dwight D. Eisenhower, with a selective admittance process and participation enshrined at the college. I graduated from the Army War College with a Master of Strategic Studies (MSS) degree.

Around 2012 I knew that I would not be selected for General Officer, and a void existed in me to fulfill my potential. That summer the University of Phoenix accepted my application to the Doctor of Management in Organizational Leadership program. That winter my mom died, and whereas most people would stop, I continued in the program to keep my mind occupied while I tried to cope with the second most devasting experience of my life: grieving for my mom. I had a great doctoral cohort who were very supportive and helped me through academically. We became great friends in the ensuing years.

In 2014 while out-processing for retirement from the Army, the University of Phoenix scholarship committee notified me that I had earned a Doctoral Leadership Scholarship. This occurred based on my essay, *Making the Grade*, which detailed the importance of my research on *Mentoring and African American Army Captain Success*. The scholarship helped pay for my Year Three Residency, which included tuition, books, and fees. The scholarship served as a great motivator and helped defray the travel cost to the Phoenix, Arizona residency site.

In 2015, I earned induction into the International Honor Society in Business for being in the top 20% of my academic class for 75% of the program. To place this in some perspective, out of every 100 doctoral program participants, only 12% graduate. That means only two in my graduating class would obtain this honor. When I arrived at the graduation ceremony, I found this to be the case.

After what seemed like forever, I finally graduated from the University of Phoenix with a Doctor of Management in Organizational Leadership. I guess the old cliché is true: "It is not how you start the race that matters, but how you finish it." I have tried to instill education in my sons and everyone I know, but I do realize that education is not for everyone. I also realize that without Dad's stern encouragement; you would not be reading this book! Even though Dad left the decision of dropping out of school to me, his lessons revealed the flaws in my thinking. Although I remained in high school, I still had a great deal to learn.

Senior Cap and Gown Picture from Paseo High School. Graduation occurred in May 1981. My largest and final afro.

RICHARD BOLLING
5TH DISTRICT, MISSOURI

COMMITTEES:
CHAIRMAN, RULES
VICE CHAIRMAN,
JOINT ECONOMIC
HOUSE DEMOCRATIC STEERING
AND POLICY

NANCY R. LOWE
ADMINISTRATIVE ASSISTANT

Congress of the United States
House of Representatives
Washington, D.C. 20515

GARY BARNES
DISTRICT DIRECTOR

KANSAS CITY OFFICE
811 GRAND AVENUE
KANSAS CITY, MISSOURI 64106
(816) 842-4798

December 23, 1980

Mr. Burl W. Randolph, Jr.
4435 Askew Avenue
Kansas City, MO 64130

Dear Burl:

After close examination of your records and qualifications,
I have the pleasure to inform you that I have today nominated
you to compete for admission to the United States Military and
Naval Academies.

These nominations are now in the hands of the proper authorities
and they will notify you shortly of further qualifying procedures
you must undertake.

Congratulations and good luck.

Sincerely,

Dick Bolling

Richard Bolling

The notifications of my congressional nominations to
WestPoint and the Naval Academy.

Inspired, Not Retired

Notes Page

CHAPTER FIFTEEN
CRITICAL THINKING: STAYING ENGAGED

"*A man ought to always stay busy.*" Burl Randolph

Some people may believe that staying busy is the premise of this book, and they would be half right. Although Dad spoke simply, he had a depth of thought I have come to appreciate over the years. Staying busy is much, much more than that modest statement conveys. I believe Dad told me about staying busy after he became sick with his first round of cancer. He explained to me all the opportunities he turned down in favor of being retired. I believe Dad was a little mad at himself for actively pursuing a seat on the sidelines of life.

THE INSIGHT

Dad conveyed to me the first opportunity he lost was managing the local bait-and-tackle business. Dad had known Mr. ZW of Z&W Bait-and-Tackle Shop in Kansas City long before I became his fishing buddy. Dad relayed when Mr. ZW said, "Burl,

I need a favor from you. How would you like to run my business for me?"

"And I remember exactly what I told him," said Dad. "'Man, are you crazy? I'm retired!'"

But Mr. ZW didn't stop there. Apparently, he pleaded with Dad, "But Burl, it wouldn't be like work. I just need you to supervise my boys. They are not quite ready yet to take over the business, and I trust you to run the business. I will pay you well."

Dad said that he did not relent and became even more surprised when the business moved because it expanded. He had no idea the worth of the business or how much money the business made, he just valued *retirement*. This was the first opportunity lost.

I believe the next opportunity lost may best be titled *Aunt Virginia*. Aunt Virginia was one of Dad's younger sisters. She was a very successful cosmetologist with Fashion Two Twenty Cosmetics. Aunt Virginia always seemed glamorous: thin, elegant, and always made-up. She conveyed that image for her job, but off the clock, I only saw her as Aunt Virginia. She loved to laugh, joke, have fun, and had a great deal of respect for my Dad. Dad visited Aunt Virginia and Aunt Edna (one of his older sisters) weekly. They lived together in a split-level duplex on 27th and Prospect in Kansas City.

After Aunt Edna died, Aunt Virginia moved into a beautiful home off 59th and The Paseo, a major thoroughfare in Kansas City. Although we did not help her move in, we spent many hours visiting her there. Being from farm country in Rural Rison, Arkansas, near Pine Bluff, the senior Randolph's (Dad and his siblings) were into gardening. Aunt Virginia had planted tomatoes in Dad's garden in the vacant lot he bought next to our home. I do not know all the details, but I know that one day while in that garden, Aunt Virginia suffered a stroke.

I was stationed at Fort Hood, Texas, at the time and only recall bits and pieces about what occurred after that. I only know what Dad told me: Aunt Virginia wanted to leave the house to him. She had only married once and had no children. The way Dad described it, she literally pleaded with him to take the house. Although the house remained in the family after Aunt Virginia died, Dad believed that he could have done more to cultivate that prime piece of real estate. This was the second opportunity lost.

THE INSPIRATION

Lastly, what I thought Dad told me exclusively, he also told my two older brothers: *"A man ought to always stay busy."*

When Dad became ill from cancer the first time, I really began to understand his thought process. The fact that he told me how he felt also did not hurt. Dad believed that his inactivity is what "helped" the cancer infect his body. Prior to that, I asked Dad what he meant behind his statement and he explained several things about men that I have found to be true:

1. **Idle hands can be the devil's workshop.** Dad believed that when men are left to their own devices, with unoccupied time on their hands, they would tend to get into trouble. *Does this describe you, your children, or your spouse?*

2. **Always be useful.** I believe that my preciseness comes from my parents. "Useful" means valuable and or beneficial, not just helpful. Helpful means obliging and/or cooperative. You can be helpful without being useful, but you cannot be useful without being helpful. *Do you add value to whatever circumstances you are in, or do you just go along to get along?*

3. **Always have a purpose.** Do not just drift through life like a sailboat without a sail. Be responsible for giving your own life meaning, regardless of what others may think or do. *Do you have a purpose? If so, what is it?*

4. **Learn to recognize opportunities.** Not every option is an opportunity, nor does every opportunity have available or reasonable options. With no monetary investment

necessary on his part, Dad regretted passing up two opportunities which would have kept him engaged daily, given him purpose, and allowed him to be useful. *Can you recognize opportunities that will allow you to remain useful?*

THE APPLICATION

I can say that I did not fully apply this principle until after Dad died. It has been both a blessing and a self-imposed curse. Because Dad fought so hard to live, I avoided eating everything I believed that killed him: eating red meat (colon cancer), smoking (although I did smoke cigars and a pipe for a time) and drinking alcohol (faith helped with this). I began to work out like a madman, became laser focused on all my tasks, and never had a free moment in my day. That last one, never a free moment in my day, became the self-imposed curse.

We all grieve differently. Because I was bound and determined to follow Dad's advice, I made the most of my time and was always involved in something. Therein lies the problem: I never relaxed. Family, work, church, school, community, whatever, I was always *doing* something to stay engaged.

I forgot another of Dad's rules until I became a Battalion Commander (CEO): Know when to rest the horses. This will be discussed later in Chapter Nineteen: Rawhide, but this principle should be applied throughout your life. For me, Inspirations one and two were easy enough to apply because I know that whenever I am idle, I do not perform at my best. It has been said that some people perform best under pressure, and unfortunately, I seem to be a pressure person. It may be because of the intellectual stimulation I receive from problem solving.

I learned to be useful by hearing two key phrases from others: He/she is just trying to be helpful. We have all heard it, and likely said it, about our small children, mate, sibling, friend, parent, coworker, or ourselves, that did something to help us that was not helpful. Remember useful versus helpful?

Friends explained the second phrase to me years later and is a southern colloquialism: Bless his/her heart. This means that a person is trying to be helpful but is any and everything but that. Having a purpose came to me in time, and I have been able to apply that principle and help share it with others. I struggled with recognizing opportunities, a likely detriment in my military career, and I am cognizant of this fact daily. Staying engaged has helped me stay inspired and not just retired. Full retirement will come soon enough.

CHAPTER SIXTEEN
INDEPENDENCE & TRUST: A TEAM SPORT

We all need other people.

If you are a parent, you understand that independence and trust are joined at the hip. To grant your child independence, you must trust that they will make the effort to do the right things. For your child to maintain their independence, they must not betray your trust. I wish these principles were listed in Parenting and Teenager 101, neither of which exist.

As you recall from Chapter Fourteen – *Education: I'm Dropping Out*, I decided to drop out of high school. Part of that decision had to do with me dating, driving, working, going to school, and the belief that I had no independence.

My mother set me straight. She explained that I came and went as I pleased without anyone questioning me. With a flair for the dramatic, she then stated, "If you were a hitman for the CIA, we would never know it. That's how much independence you have."

Being utterly speechless, it was more so because my mom knew who the CIA were! Now, I am not saying our Central Intelligence Agency has hitmen or that my life was shrouded in secrecy, but mom wanted to point out the great degree of freedom I had. I was independent. Dad was a tougher sell on that idea.

THE INSIGHT

As a poor college student, I had no money other than the $100 a month stipend I received from participating in the SROTC. My full scholarship paid for tuition, books, fees, room, and board. Other than that, I was a poor college student. This line of thinking played well while in military school, but once Dad started paying my tuition, I had to account for every penny. "The first rule of independence," he told me, "is realizing that you must sometimes depend on other people."

THE INSPIRATION

Dad's logic about independence defied me at every level. How could independence involve depending on other people? Independence should mean freedom from other people, right? As a young Second Lieutenant my own thought process contradicted my training on building teams. At the time I served in the Army

Reserves and lacked exposure to the Active Army daily inculcation of management, leadership, and teambuilding. This should have been my first clue: When we work independent of others for prolonged periods, we forget the necessity of serving with others.

As I mentioned in a blog I wrote on my website, mywingmanllc.com, "I have not engaged in many endeavors alone."[33] I believe my thought processes had also changed after transferring from a small military school in the mid-west, Kemper Military School and College, to the massive four year institution of Iowa State University. Although I had friends, worked at several jobs, and co-owned a small business called Cover to Cover Comics, my thoughts on teamwork had gone astray. Anyone who has issues with trust, independence, and teamwork should ask themselves a few questions:

1. **What have I ever accomplished alone?** My SROTC scholarships and academy nominations were not accomplished alone. MSG Scott, my military mentor, initiated my scholarship to Kemper, so I did not even begin that process alone! *What substantive accomplishments have you ever achieved alone?*

2. **How do I work with others?** I strive to work well with others and to be a coordinator, collaborator, and communicator, although that may not always be the case

for various reasons (e.g., off day, project lead, short suspense, etc.). *Are you the coworker you believe you are?*

3. **Do I work better with others or alone?** I believe we all *think* that we work better alone, but I hate being embarrassed by mistakes that could have been avoided. Although I write well, I must have an editor because as I have been told, "You can think faster than you can type." This means that my thoughts may be incomplete on paper and leave the reader wondering because of gaps. Remember, even the Lone Ranger was a misnomer. He had Tonto! *How do you work best?*

4. **When on a team, how do others see me?** How I see myself as a teammate may be quite different from how my coworkers see me. Am I a trusted teammate or too independent? *What would coworkers and peers say about how you work with them?*

5. **Am I a team player or an instigator?** Some people are not team players. In some instances that is fine. However, some people want to instigate drama by troubleshooting and undermining the team. *Are you a team player or instigator?*

Depending on other people may be a learned skill for some. For me, this became a lesson learned about independence and trust that I would have never imagined.

THE APPLICATION

The financial aid system for higher education has always been fraught with problems. Even when you think you have done everything correctly; human error can overturn all your hard efforts. The proverb "No good deed goes unpunished" is the antithesis of the idea that good people are rewarded for being good. In the following instance, it felt like a punishment.

It was the Spring of 1985. I had just taken an unwanted academic sabbatical and was ready to work. At this point, I was paying for my own education in full: No Dad-Help-Me fund, and no scholarships or GI Bill. Just good old-fashioned grants. The rules had changed from what seemed like unlimited government support to "parents should be able to help their students until age 24." My financial aid request had been submitted and approved prior to that new "law," so I was grandfathered in. I was waiting in line to pick up my $2500 grant check for my tuition, books, and fees and then had planned to be on my way.

The student clerk at the financial aid window told me that the check could not be disbursed because I had not submitted a copy of my federal income tax return. "Impossible", I said. I prided myself on submitting my paperwork on time, especially my income tax returns. Impossible as that may seem, no tax return, no grant check. As I smugly returned to my apartment, confident that

I would just find my tax return, return to finance, and submit it, guess what? I could not find a copy of my tax return anywhere! After about an hour of searching, I gave up and decided that I would just fill out the paperwork again. That turned out to be a tremendous mistake. Remember, there was no internet to download a copy from the Internal Review Service (IRS). I had no time to contact them because my tuition payment was required in three days!

As I filled out my tax forms, I noticed that I had incorrectly stated my income. That seemed odd because the IRS always told me when I made a mistake. Oh well, it's just for the University, so I completed the paperwork, returned to the financial aid office and turned it in right before closing. When I returned for my check the next day, $2500 had been reduced to $250!

After regaining my composure from almost fainting I asked the clerk, "What is the meaning of this?" She replied that based on my tax return, I made too much money and my eligibility dropped to only $250. Long story shorter, my original tax return had been misplaced by someone in the financial aid office and found later, but the university could only use "The latest information submitted." My anger caused me not to see straight. That more than likely also explains why I check and recheck things so often. Although losing paperwork may be acceptable for the average person, the cost of such inefficiency to me created an extraordinary and devasting event. To resolve this, I knew what I had to do.

Only Dad had the amount of money I needed in such a short period of time. The phone call home was awkward at best, and I fumbled through explaining the situation of why I needed the money.

"How much do you need?" Dad asked.

"Twenty-two hundred," I said.

"Oh," Dad said, "That might take me a couple of days to get together."

I was shocked but immediately said, "Don't worry about it, dad. I will get it. Don't worry about it."

Dad then asked, "Tell me again how much you need?"

I replied, "Twenty-two hundred."

"Two thousand, two hundred dollars?" he asked.

Confused I said, "Yes, two thousand, two hundred dollars."

Dad began to laugh, which confused me even more. He said, "I thought you said '$22,000.' I'll send the check in the mail today."

I was elated!!!—for about 30 seconds. We said our goodbyes and hung up the phone. Then I realized what had just happened: my dad was going to give me $22,000 because he thought that I asked for it! Think about this for a moment. He was going to send $22,000 to a college student whose academics he no longer supported monetarily. I never asked Dad about this, or questioned his responses, but even today I am in awe of two things:

1. **Dad's definition of independence came to fruition**. Not only did Dad's definition come to fulfillment, I benefitted from it. I needed help and *depended* on him to help me, although I claimed independence.

2. **Dad trusted me implicitly**. This event is the best example I can think of to illustrate trust because this conversation was never spoken about. Dad and I never talked about this, it was years before I told mom, and this information is relatively new to my siblings. The reason I wrote "implicitly" was because there was no real reservation or mention of repayment.

There was no way I could have predicted that someone else's mistake would cause dire consequences for me. The situation forced me to swallow my pride, open my eyes, and fully recognize that independence and trust are a team sport. I was so happy to have learned that lesson because as a family, we would need to be the strongest team possible for the next series of events that would occur. The situation demanded strength, trust, and fearlessness.

My first year at Iowa State University, Fall 1983. I thought I was Superman, but my grades did not reflect it!

Second Lieutenant Randolph standing next to his Jeep in September 1984. I was with the 372nd Engineer Group as the Liaison Officer to 7th US Corps for Return Forces to Germany (REFORGER) Exercise.

Notes Page

CHAPTER SEVENTEEN
FEARLESSNESS: FIGHT BACK

Fearlessness: Acting despite being afraid.

Cancer only has one address: To Whom It May Concern. Sometimes despite all we do in eating right, getting enough sleep, and living generally healthy, we or someone we know may be infected with cancer. This happened to our family in 1987, the year I graduated from Iowa State University and was selected to enter Active Duty.

Graduating with a Bachelor of Science in General Business was great and being part of the 40% selected from the Army Reserves for Active Duty was awesome. But nothing could have prepared me for what would happen during that Thanksgiving weekend.

Dad had been sick for what seemed like a while. At first, we just thought it was a cold, and then possibly pneumonia, but both would have been an early start to the cold and flu season. Finally, Dad went to the hospital and was diagnosed with cancer.

He was scheduled for a "routine" surgery the week before Thanksgiving. I had orders to report to Fort Sill, Oklahoma, to attend the Officer Basic Course (OBC) for Field Artillery with a report date of November 17th. Both Mom and Dad suggested that I go on, and I knew that I could return home for Thanksgiving break. Easy-peezy-lemon-squeezy, right? Boy, were we ever wrong!

Sometime the Friday after I departed, Dad had taken a turn for the worse and the cancer threatened to close off his airway. With Dad, Mom, and my sister Teresa as the driver, they raced from the doctor's office to the hospital. According to our parents, Teresa must have had special dispensation from the Kansas City Police Department to run every red light, stop sign, or any other inconsequential traffic signal to get Dad to the hospital!

Teresa's actions likely saved his life, and we were grateful that she had that true Randolph Spirit of defying authority and doing what she thought was right. Trust me, that part of the Randolph Spirit got me into trouble plenty of times.

When I arrived at Fort Sill, Oklahoma, I had been assigned a dorm room, was in-processed for classes, had taken a PT (Physical Fitness test), and was assigned to remedial PT for missing the run time by 17 seconds. Wow, I was seven hours from home, in the middle of nowhere, trying to make new friends, and already excelling by doing PT twice a day. Could it get any better? No, it could not and did not. All of this occurred during my first three to four duty days there, so I was unprepared when I got back from class and there was an urgent message to call home.

I went to the payphone (no cell phones back then) and called home. "What's up mom?" I said.

Mom immediately began to lay into me for not calling home sooner. "Mom, I just got your message. What's the big deal?" I asked.

"Your father's having surgery in the morning and I sent the Red Cross message seven hours ago!"

I was stunned! I told her that I was on the way, but she told me to wait and come in the morning. It would be 7pm before I hit the road, and they were concerned about my safety. "I'll be there," I said.

Furious, I went to the orderly room and said rather loudly, "WHERE'S THE FIRST SERGEANT!" Because I was a First Lieutenant, I was expected to set the example for the class, and boy, was I about to set one! I planned to make an example out of the First Sergeant, who strenuously told us during in-processing, "If you have a family emergency, do not just leave or you will be charged as AWOL—Absent Without Official Leave. If you receive a Red Cross message, I will have you out of here in two hours." At this point, that was all blah, blah, blah to me, and I demanded to know what happened. The First Sergeant was frazzled because I was pissed off and he had royally screwed up!

The First Sergeant had the S1 (Human Resources) complete an emergency leave form for me, he signed it, and sent me on my way. I only had to pack a couple of items for the trip back home because OBC was considered TDY (Temporary Duty), so most of my things remained in Kansas City. I jumped in my brand-new Oldsmobile Calais GT and roared up the highway for home.

THE INSIGHT

I arrived home at 2am. Dad's surgery was scheduled for 7am. Mom told me to get some sleep and come to the hospital later. Around 10am the phone ringing woke me up. It was the American Red Cross checking to see if the Service Member had arrived. I told them I had, and what time I had gotten there. After a long pause, the caller asked, "Sir, what time were you notified by your unit that you had a Red Cross message?"

"Seventeen hundred", I answered. That is 5pm in civilian language.

"What?" she screamed into the phone. "We left the message at 11am! Why did it take them six hours to notify you?"

I had no idea, and she assured me that an investigation would be launched.

Since I was awake, I figured I may as well get cleaned up and go to the hospital. When I arrived at the hospital, everyone looked glum. I asked, "Where's Dad?"
My mother replied, "He's still in surgery."

Just being myself, I asked, "Why?" I am certain that question seemed stupid to my family, until they thought about it. When I went out and asked the nurse the status of the Randolph surgery, she went and found out.

When the doctor arrived after surgery, he provided a simple explanation, "Mr. Randolph has a larger frame then most men his age, and we underestimated the amount of time it would take." Dr. Maslon went on to say that, "The surgery was successful, and he should be out of recovery within the hour." A larger frame equated to having a barrel chest.

The next few weeks were strenuous to say the least. The only one not in Kansas City was me, but I was there mentally. The next decision came when the doctor indicated Dad needed something called radiation to ensure the cancer did not return from the difficult to cut areas. Not knowing much about radiation versus chemotherapy, the family decided that Dad should not undergo the treatments. They elected me to discuss this with my Dad. Oh, the benefits of being absent and volunteered!

Well, the conversation was a short one. I explained to Dad how the family felt, and that he should not have the treatments. I asked what he thought about what I had said. His response was a short, sweet, and simple one:

"No."

I asked was it, "No, you were not having the treatments?" He shook his head **No**. He did not agree with our recommendation. Because he was using a speech apparatus at the time, his words were few but carefully crafted.

"You won't blame me," he said.

"Blame you for what?" I asked.

Dad went on to say, "You won't blame me after I die by saying, 'He didn't do all he could to live.' You won't blame me."

There you have it. I relayed it to the family as he relayed it to me. Although I did not fully understand what he meant at the time, I understood one thing: He was going to fight back the cancer to live. It did not matter what we said, how we felt, or what we thought, he would follow the doctor's recommendation for radiation treatments. We were glad that he overruled our recommendation because the treatments were successful and without any significant side effects. This taught me that sometimes you must fight back, regardless of the circumstances, your feelings, your fears, or the feelings of others. I also learned that there is a method to successfully fighting back.

THE INSPIRATION

Dad's one-word response and subsequent explanation told me what he had told me all my life: Fight Back.

Even if you are raised in the best home imaginable, full of peace, harmony, joy, and laughter, at some point in life you will be required to *Fight Back*. Fighting back may involve the bully at school, church, work, in your neighborhood, or on social media. Fighting back may be against stereotypes such as racism, sexism, and body shaming. Fighting back may be against those in your family or friends that may seek to harm you. Fighting back may be against the insecurities in your own mind that keep you paralyzed with fear. Whatever the situation, sometimes we must *Fight Back*.

Dad was determined to Fight Back from his cancer. It was a bigger fight than any of us expected, but none of us had ever undergone extensive surgery either. Only Dad knew and could explain his limitations. Because of the surgery and recuperation, his strength had deteriorated dramatically. I learned this when we went fishing for the first time about six months after the surgery. It was an unseasonably warm spring, so we decided to do what we loved, go fishing. As we approached the first fishing spot, I noticed that Dad was struggling. He told me that he was not the same and needed to catch his breath. I realized that Dad was fighting back much harder than any of us knew to regain his strength.

Through many conversations during Dad's recovery period, I learned several things about Fighting Back:

1. **Know what you are fighting for**. Dad knew that he was first fighting for his life, then to regain his health and strength after the surgery. Because he was the "Man in the Arena," as Teddy Roosevelt put it, [34] he had the best perspective on what he was fighting for. *What are you fighting for? Love, peace, respect, joy, happiness, or your very life? Do you even know?*

2. **Know what it takes to win**. Not all fights are winnable. Some would say, "Then why fight, if you cannot win?" Until you are in the fight, you may not know if the fight is winnable. This was my family's first experience with cancer. We did not know the stages of cancer; the doctor was extremely positive that he had removed all traces of the cancer and that Dad would have a full recovery. Dad had faith that this was a winnable fight, but faith is in the next chapter. *Do you know what it takes to win your fight? Is it the battle of the bulge, crabby coworkers,*

lackadaisical leadership, or finicky finances? What does it take to win?

3. **Fight a real challenge, not just a philosophical one**. Some people just like to fight. Statistically, no matter how good you are, everyone loses a fight or two, so make the battle worth it. Dad had no point to prove, because the fight was not philosophical, but for real. *Is your fight real or in principle? Does the principle impede a moral imperative? Or is it just to make you feel better? Or is it just because you like to fight?*

4. **Gather your support systems to help in the fight**. Dad knew that he was not in the condition he was before the surgery and let me know it on our fishing trip. He was gathering his support system to help him fight. That required me to adjust my thinking and my actions. Sometimes I needed to be the strength he did not have, the voice he could no longer use, and carry the load of responsibility for this trip. *Do you have a support system to help you in your fight? Family, friends, finances, faith, intellect, free resources may all be your support system.*

5. **Know what the Milestones are to victory.** A milestone is a momentous breakthrough achieved in a project or event. Dad knew that one of his milestones was to regain

his strength. This took nearly nine months after the surgery and subsequent treatments. He also had other milestones, many of which he needed a support system to accomplish. *What are your milestones to victory?*

6. **Define success.** Success does not define itself. Success must be defined by the person or organization that is pursuing it. Regaining his strength was one of Dad's definitions of success. *How do you define success?*

7. **Know the limitations and delimitations.** Dad knew his limitations physically because of the surgery—things he could not do. Dad also knew his delimitations—things he *chose* not to do. While Dad spoke with the aid of a device, a limitation, he never went hunting again, a delimitation. *Do you know your limitations and delimitations?*

8. **Accept a graceful surrender.** Sometimes we fight for how things used to be. That is normally not possible, which makes it unwinnable. Dad wanted to be able to still work in his garden, get around on his own, and enjoy the things that he could. His definitions for success were simple, and he accepted them gracefully. *Are you still fighting for an unconditional surrender, after you have already achieved success?*

9. **Reestablish boundaries.** Once victory is achieved, boundaries must be reestablished. Without new boundaries, victories are subject to relapses in our gains. *What boundaries have you reestablished after your victory?*

10. **Move on when you have achieved your success.** Once you have attained your victory, move on. Reveling in a victory from years ago is basically living in the past. After boundaries were reestablished, we learned to help Dad enjoy his life in a new way. *Have you moved on to the next event, or are you still living in the past of how it used to be?*

This may seem like a lengthy list, but it is only because fighting back and being successful are hard work. There is no easy path to success, recovery, or fighting back. I soon found that out.

THE APPLICATION

This is the only chapter in the book where the Insight, Inspiration, and Application create a contiguous story. The Application covers how I had to Fight Back to remain on Active Duty during this period. I labeled my three fights as *AWOL, Disaster*, and *Academic Review Board.*

Active Duty had lost its luster based on the events surrounding Dad's illness and what followed. When I returned to

Fort Sill after Dad's surgery, I was greeted with less than a warm reception. Our Platoon Leader, Second Lieutenant Christopher Stolz, took me to the side after Monday morning PT formation and asked, "Where have you been?"

He was deadly serious, and I sort of laughed it off and asked, "You're kidding, right?"

He replied no, and that I was being carried as AWOL since the previous Wednesday.

"Yah, right," I replied. "Let's go running."

"You need to go see the Battery Commander, ASAP," he said. "This is serious."

I left, went back to my dorm, put on my uniform, and headed for the orderly room.

When I arrived at the orderly room, there were darted eyes and glances as if one of America's Most Wanted had just walked in. "I'm here to see the Battery Commander," I said. Everyone seemed to know why I was there, but the Battery Commander, Captain Wendall, was not in. I was told that I needed to come back at lunchtime. Oh well, a waste of a good PT day, so I went and had breakfast.

When I attended classes, every instructor asked me the same question: "Where have you been, Lieutenant?" Now I knew how *The Fugitive* felt, except I was also the one-armed man. Look it up. You will enjoy the story. Fortunately for me, we had a class on the Uniform Code of Military Justice (UCMJ) right before lunch, and the lawyers did not know me.

AWOL

We could ask the Judge Advocate General (JAG) lawyers questions in private, and I provided a hypothetical about being charged as AWOL but being in possession of a signed DA 31— Department of the Army Leave Form. The response was that if the person who signed the leave form had the authority to approve leave, the leave holder (which was me in this case) was golden.

Armed with that knowledge, I went to see the Battery Commander. Once again, the orderly room was like Tombstone, and I felt like Doc Holliday without Wyatt Earp and his brothers. Captain Wendall walked out of his office and escorted me to the lounge outside his office. Captain Wendall was a gentle man, a Mormon, and in the short time we had seen him, we never saw him upset or heard him raise his voice.

He asked where I had been, who told me I could go, and if I knew that I was being carried as AWOL. When I told him that I was on emergency leave, and that the First Sergeant had known about it, Captain Wendall said there was no proof. I pulled out a leave form signed by the First Sergeant. At that exact moment who should show up? The First Sergeant! When Captain Wendall questioned him about the leave form, the First Sergeant answered in a cavalier manner. When the Commander asked, "Why wasn't I informed?" the First Sergeant responded, "What's the big deal?"

That was the wrong answer, as Captain Wendall raised his voice, locked the First Sergeants heels (ordered him to the position of Attention), and reminded him who the Commander was! Even I was a little shaken! He ordered the First Sergeant into his office and apologized to me profusely. When I went to the S-1 to validate my leave form, the Specialist could not find it. Asking the Personnel Sergeant, he told me that he did not know what I was talking about. He said they knew where I was and why, and that I was never carried as AWOL.

Based on my interactions with the First Sergeant, this could have tainted my perception of the Army noncommissioned officer (NCO) corps. The NCOs in the S-1 however, knew the First Sergeant had not lived up to his end of the bargain on my Red Cross message. They took care of me so that I did not become disgruntled. Fortunately, after that day, we never saw the First Sergeant again. I was redeemed with the faculty and my classmates. All the redemption in the world, however, could not deter my desire to be home, and it showed in my performance.

From Disaster to Redemption

I have always been a decent student with acceptable study habits leading to exceptional grades. By February 1988, however, I just did not care. Christmas was tough with Dad still ill, I had fought the AWOL charges, and had injured my wrist trying to break a fall while running on ice. Yes, we were required to conduct PT in those conditions. Something else the new Battery Commander had to deal with. I was able to sufficiently pass my classes and the test because the subjects were nothing new.

Once we entered Gunnery however, it was a new day. Gunnery was the technical aspects of getting the artillery round out of the howitzer tube and onto the target with accuracy and timeliness. It was tough, but it seemed like I shuffled through the classroom work with acceptable grades. The TFT (Tactical Fires Trainer), however, would expose my shortcomings.

In short, I could not correctly Call for Fire on this system to save my life. A Call for Fire is what a forward observer uses to request artillery fire on an enemy target. I was so bad on the TFT, I had secretly referred to myself as Wrong Way Randolph. Whenever the rounds needed to be adjusted to hit the target, I sent them the wrong way.

My only redemption was the JAAT (Joint Air Attack Target) exercise we were required to participate in. A JAAT is when a target that is difficult to kill such as a Soviet T-72 tank, is engaged with artillery fires, an attack helicopter, and an A-10 Air Force fighter. Our class had secured an A-10 Warthog (the nickname for the fighter) for the exercise, and live rounds would be expended! The A-10 was referred to as the Warthog because it looked slow and cumbersome, like a warthog. However, when it attacked, it was deadly accurate, like an attacking warthog!

Our Gunnery Instructor shouted, "First Lieutenant Randolph, you're up."

You could have heard a mouse pee on a cotton ball as I approached the RTO (Radio-Telephone Operator) and took the hand microphone. "Just follow the script," said the Instructor.

What came next shocked everyone, especially me. I vectored the A-10 into position, authorized the Request to Engage Target and **BOOM-BOOM-BOOM,** a direct hit on the target! In Charlie Brown fashion, I handed the mic back to the RTO, walked back to my position, and never said a word.

"Now that's what I'm talking about," said the Instructor. "I didn't think it was me. Apparently, SOMEBODY was listening in class. Let's go gentlemen."

The Gunnery Instructor was a cocky Marine First Lieutenant named Sartor, and he had reason to be cocky: He was the only Lieutenant Instructor in the entire Gunnery Department! 1LT Sartor came over to me and said, "Good job. I need to see you in my office after class."

"Sure-thing," I said, and continued to enjoy the rest of my day. I was the first one from our group to hit the target. Redemption tasted sweet but had a bitter aftertaste.

Academic Review Board

When I arrived at 1LT Sartor's office, I was still flying high about my JAAT experience. Although Sartor and I were both 1LTs, he never referred to me or anyone else by their first name. After two or three months, he was breaking character. "Dude, WTF?" he said. For the uninitiated, *WTF* means *What the Freak?* to put it cleanly. I knew what he was talking about because on the TFT, I had a perfect score: 0.

"How in the world can you call in an A-10 and hit the target, but not do it in class?" he asked.

"I guess because it's real," I said.

"What?" Sartor said.

I replied, "The classroom stuff is not real, so I guess I could not visualize it. The A-10 was real, so I could engage with it."

"Dude, you know we do six fires exercises and I drop the lowest score, so you need to kill the next three to pass," he told me.

Unfortunately, I only killed two of the next three, and when your lowest score is zero, times four, it kills the vibe. Academic Review Board (ARB), here I come!

I was not happy. This area in gunnery drove down my entire GPA below the 70-points thresholds for academic standards, so I was placed on academic hold pending the board results. This meant that I could not participate in any activities beyond fighting to stay in class.

There was another African American officer facing the same board, and oddly enough, they saw us together. There was only one substantive question: "Why should we retain you in the class?"

My answer was simple: "My performance on the TFT was not indicative of my abilities." I went on to say, "The early TFTs were a snapshot in time where I could not visualize the screen as the battlefield. The JAAT proved that I could perform in a real scenario."

I believe that we were both approved for retention. The proof of the board results to external parties was participation in the end of course live-fire exercises. I participated and had a blast.

I thought that November 1987 through May 1988 would be the most difficult period of my life, at least in the Army. I had avoided charges of being AWOL, redeemed myself academically, and won against the ARB. Although I still struggled with one other frailty: being overweight, I had fought back on the other three occasions, and won. I would have to fight back throughout the next 28 years on Active Duty, sometimes for myself and sometimes for others.

Once you learn how to fight back it does not become easier, just manageable. I would need those skills as I entered the world of Field Artillery, Fort Hood, Texas, racism, and combat.

This blurry picture of me in front of an M109A3 howitzer was my redemption. It showed that I was beat the Academic Review Board and participated in the End of Course Exercise.

Notes Page

CHAPTER EIGHTEEN
FAITH: A COMBAT MULTIPLIER

"So, you do the best you can and don't forget to pray."
Burl Randolph

Religion or spirituality may be a large part of most African Americans heritage. I chose to make that gross generalization because most of my African American friends, relatives, and even some enemies have told me the same thing: "Sometimes all you have is your faith." Although Dad took mom to church, he rarely attended.

According to our Uncle Joe, aka Reverend J.B. Randolph, one of my Dad's younger brothers, everyone thought that Dad would be the preacher in the family. Uncle Joe would say, "When we were growing up in Arkansas, your Dad could preach up a storm!" All my aunts and uncles affirmed it, so we had no choice but to believe it, right?

At some point in time all seven of us, three boys and four girls, attended Gethsemane Baptist Church, which Uncle Joe led as our pastor. My mom attended St. John Missionary Baptist Church because, I believe, she was attending that church when she met my Dad. Throughout my middle and high school years, we attended church every Sunday morning. The 'We' were me and my younger sisters, Debora and Alisa. Our family was sort of divided into two camps: Old Heads and New Meat, as I've since come to think of it. My elder siblings, Lynn Toni, Sterling, Larry, and Teresa composed the Old Heads, so we were the New Meat.

THE INSIGHT

Dad never spoke much about religion, but when he did, he could quote bible scriptures and knew what it meant like nobody's business. I made this qualification because anyone can quote scripture, but to know what it means at a level that others can understand is an art. As I was employed cutting the church grass, selling fish dinners, or attending Vacation Bible School, Dad always supported us. He never stopped us from attending any church event, and I am certain he encouraged it just to get us out of the house. It was not until I was attending Iowa State University that Dad chose to breach the subject of religion.

Dad would always come back to my room, which was in the very back of the house, to have those in-depth conversations. I try that with my sons, unless I am feeling lazy. Then, I just send them a text to "Come see me" or "Let's chat." Dad asked me if I was attending church at college. I responded, "*Sometimes.*" Apparently, I was not very convincing.

"Son," Dad said, "you need to have Christ in your life. You never know when you might need Him."

All I did was nod in agreement and said that I would look harder to find a church while in college. That was the end of the conversation as Dad left the room and left me with something to think about.

THE INSPIRATION

Dad gave me something to think about. Although I joined church at around the age of 13, I was not baptized. When I asked, 'Why do I need to be baptized if I believe?" I felt the explanations were insufficient, so I did not do it. Remember earlier when I mentioned having a contrary spirit? Yes, this was just another example. Hearing what Dad told me was a bit different than hearing it in church. No hardline or sales pitch, as some people call it, just a statement of what I discovered later was fact.

When I returned to Iowa State from my visit home, I began in earnest looking for a place to worship. There was a Gospel Group on campus that met every other Sunday. I thought, *Perfect!* Well, every other Sunday turned into whenever space was available. I lost interest in attending, but not in my faith.

My faith was next inspired by bottoming out my car in a ravine during a snowstorm after spinning out on the highway. I drove out of the channel and continued to school without injuries but with a badly damaged car, which I did not fully discover until the Spring.

My faith was tested and strengthened again when I switched from Architecture to Business. My well-orchestrated plan to become an architect was not willy-nilly. I took the pre-requisite classes in high school and junior college and had decent grades in the numerous drafting and art courses, algebra, trigonometry, and calculus. The "other" classes, i.e., English, sciences, and foreign language, were what I considered "easy" or the "soft" classes. And then there was my bread-and-butter class: SROTC. My college degree was just the means to becoming an Active Duty officer.

Iowa State University College of Design was new, untested, but no joke. I soon discovered that I did not draw any better than I sang, but now it was showing. Even after receiving tutoring every day in Architecture 145, its companion class, Architecture 146, is what killed me. Although I had recently learned that all architects were not Frank Lloyd Wright, and the entry level pay was squat, a technical term for Not Much, it was the lack of talent that convinced me.

At this juncture, I was a commissioned officer serving in the US Army Reserve Corps of Engineers. This was how serious I was about architecture. I am assuming after all these years it was God who spoke to me and said, "It's time." It was time to face the unpleasant truth that architecture would not be my career field in any way, shape, or form after seven years of trying (four years in high school, three years in college). I believe without my faith, it would have been easy to quit and drop out of college, but the stakes were too high.

Remember the Two-Year TRADOC Dedicated Army ROTC Scholarship I won to Kemper Military School and College? Well, scholarships were not passed out like candy. I had made friends from the small scholarship recipient pool, six or seven, half of which dropped out of school and lost the scholarship.

My quandary was that I had not dropped out but graduated with an Associate of Arts degree and was commissioned a Second Lieutenant. A stipulation of the contract was that I would complete my baccalaureate education, serve on Active Duty for four years, and then serve two years in the Army Reserves. Failure to achieve any part of the contract unless by unforeseen circumstances was considered a breach of contract, and I would have had to repay ALL scholarship monies received!

Because I attended a military school and the scholarship paid for tuition, books, fees, room, board, and my military training,

I was likely looking at $20–30,000 in 1985 dollars. The year the dollars were calculated is almost irrelevant since I did not have the money anyway. I had to find a way to persevere and "Soldier on," as Soldiers say. Although architecture was tough, I did not have the skills to compete, so I returned to my first true love and one that would allow me to eventually graduate: business.

I felt like God had guided me through those events, so I was on Easy Street, right? Wrong! Oh, I was so wrong. Between switching majors, being heavily involved with the Army Reserves, and attaining a newfound freedom from drawing every day, I may have begun to slack up a little and party a lot! Long story short: I was invited to sit out a semester to reprioritize my objectives. Oh, the shame of it all!

Fortunately, I convinced the Dean of the College of Business to sign me into a class that was full, and that allowed me to return the following semester. Although he gave me credit for my ingenuity in coming to him, and I could bypass the Academic Review Board process necessary for reinstatement, he required me to sit out the semester.

The Dean began with, "Burl, I reviewed your academic record at military school." He continued, "Scholarship recipient, Army Lieutenant, and more than capable." Now came the cold, hard, truth: "But, you have not performed at that level here at Iowa State." The consequences: "I believe you need to sit out the semester and think about what you need to do to succeed and graduate."

After informing my parents (who I am certain told the rest of the family) and telling my job (so that I could work more hours), I began the arduous task of reflection, faith finding, and determining my course. God had opened more doors than I had closed, and it was up to me to continue walking through them if I wanted to succeed. I did return to school, became a "B" student, and did eventually graduate one semester later than I had projected.

The faith that the Dean showed in me by not causing me to endure the gauntlet (ARB) to return to college provided the faith I needed to press forward. This small inconvenience was only the beginning of my faith journey.

THE APPLICATION

Life moves at a breakneck pace. I graduated from Iowa State and was selected for Active Duty from the Army Reserves, one of the few who were selected that year from the 40% throughout the United States. The problem in 1987 was the same problem it is now: the federal budget. Because the appropriations and approval processes were so slow, and the services were playing catch-up, all non-Service Academy selections for Active Duty were moved to the next fiscal year. This meant that I needed a job for six months while waiting to go on Active Duty. Those six months were easy. The next four years were tough.

As I mentioned previously, I entered Active Duty in November 1987 and was only there a week when the Red Cross message came in about Dad going into emergency surgery. This would be the first major crisis that impacted our entire immediate family, and where our faith would be tested. I struggled through the Field Artillery Officers Basic Course (OBC) at Fort Sill, Oklahoma, wondering if I should stay. I had no reason not too, and over the course of the next four years would return to Kansas City, Missouri, often. I was assigned to Fort Hood, Texas, at the time, and I drove home to see how my mom and dad were doing with the circumstances that created a different life.

Things seemed almost normal until 1989, when Dad was diagnosed with another type of cancer. This was a bit more strenuous on him because he was 75 years old. As with the previous cancer, not much was said about it, we just adjusted, learned how to help Mom help Dad, and continued to live life. I was still driving back and forth from Fort Hood on the four-day weekends because there were no cellphones, Skype, Facetime, Facebook, or any other way to see my parents.

The following year, 1990, proved monumental and extremely stressful in our lives. Saddam Hussein was saber rattling, and President George H.W. Bush took his threats seriously. I also married Terry Lynn Lee from Lincoln University, Pennsylvania. We became engaged in August 1990, right after the Iraqi Army invaded Kuwait.

"Big deal" I thought, "What does that have to do with me?" I soon found out as the 1st Cavalry Division was activated for deployment. Although the wedding was planned for nine months later in May 1991, the deployment timetable moved that forward.

What could be done later was done sooner, and we were married in August 1990. I shipped out in October 1990, six days after my birthday. In Saudi Arabia before the hostilities began, we were allotted three minutes a week (or maybe it was a month) to call the US, courtesy of AT&T. Because I was married, I called Terry and had her relay my condition to the rest of my family. During my second deployment to Iraq in 2003, we had advanced communications to email, albeit on a shared unclassified terminal with several others.

By 2008, my last Iraq deployment, I could call back to the states using a calling card practically anytime. Because of the time difference, however, we still needed a calling schedule, but I was able to talk with our two sons and call my mom.

Mail call was always the biggest thing during any military deployment because it was your main connection with home. In 1990, after completing our Thanksgiving feast, SCUD rockets were launched the next day. At the next mail call, I received a letter with my Dad's address label for the return address. It read like this:

> *Nov 28-19-90*
>
> *Dear Son,*
>
> *How are you? Fine, I hope. How is everything over there? Hope you are doing OK. Well, everything is doing fine here. The weather is fine. Well, how do you get along with the boys? Are you the boss?*
>
> *Well, I can't write much. My hands shake so bad but hope you can read it. I don't know much to say. Haven't wrote in so long. So, you do the best you can and don't forget to pray. So long for now.*
>
> *Your Dad   Burl*

This is the only letter I ever knew my father to write. His hand shook because of his Parkinson's Disease, but he was determined to write his son in combat. My mom sent a letter in the same envelope and provided me the news on all my siblings, my nieces and nephews, and her correspondence with Terry. Her letter was much longer, and she was not at a loss for words.

I still have the letter Dad wrote me with a small memorial I maintain for him in my home, no matter where I live. The memorial is composed of the things Dad seemed to love the most: horses. I added the Buffalo Soldier memorabilia once it became the craze.

On his birthday in 1988, I gave Dad artist Don Stiver's first Buffalo Soldier print, *Tracking Victorio,* symbolizing the 10th US Cavalry Regiment. Dad was proud to hang it in the living room and spoke a bit more about his military service after that. Mom gave me the print after Dad died.

After six months I made it home from my first combat deployment. After shaking off the dust, Terry and I traveled to Kansas City to see the family. I could see that Dad was not doing well but was keeping the faith. By then, I was actively pursuing my faith while trying to adjust to being back in the USA, being a husband, and decompressing after combat. Although home safe and sound in the confines of the US, my faith would be supremely tested later in 1991.

Notes Page

CHAPTER NINETEEN
COMPASSION & LOYALTY: MY PEOPLE

Always take care of your people.

It was time. It was late September 1991, and Dad had been sick from cancer for over four years. When Terry handed me the phone and said it was my mom, I knew it was time. Back then, Mom only called when there was a problem.

"Your father is back in the hospital, and I don't know what to do," she said.

"Do we need to come home?" I asked.

"Yes," she replied.

I called my supervisor to let him know that I needed to take emergency leave. The thing about being an officer and a leader, rarely can you just drop what you are doing. When I called the airlines to book the flights, they asked if I was military and I said "Yes." I remembered that the last troops from Operation Desert Storm had only been back home for a couple of months, and the country was still high on the military victory in Iraq. My tickets were discounted, so now all I had to do was get through the next day.

Since my issue with the Army over a delayed Red Cross message and emergency leave in 1987, I was very sensitive to the emergency leave process. I was currently assigned as the Battalion S2 (Chief Intelligence Officer) for the 3rd Battalion of the 82nd Field Artillery, 1st Cavalry Division, and back then we were preparing for an event even greater than war—a Nuclear Surety Certification. In short, I was the "keeper of the codes" for the battalion tactical nuke employment, so if my section got it wrong, nothing else much mattered with the inspection. My crew and my boss told me not to worry and just go take care of my father. Although normally I would drive the 11 hours to Kansas City, Missouri, something told me to fly.

THE INSIGHT

When we arrived in Kansas City the following day, we went to my parents' home and then to the hospital. I was scheduled to be home for a couple of weeks at least and hoped for the best, regardless of the situation. I would visit the hospital everyday: once in the morning and once in the afternoon or evening. Dad looked good despite the situation, and always seemed happy to see me.

The reason I went twice a day is because I would normally go prior to working out in the morning, running three to four miles at Jacob Loose Park. When I went back in the afternoon or evening, Terry, my wife, would go with me. The mornings were my "alone time" with Dad, considering our large family of seven children and Dad still having several siblings, nieces, and nephews throughout the city who would visit him throughout the day. It is a wonder he got any rest!

October was fast approaching, and it was a few days before my birthday when I went to see Dad one morning. He looked particularly tired and a bit off. I am uncertain what we were talking about, but I remember him saying, "I don't want to go." He was very sad as he said it, and I thought I knew what he meant, but asked my typical "Why?" question anyway. He looked at me, heartfelt, and said,

"Because I don't want to leave my people."

I instinctively knew that Dad was talking about us, his family, that he loved, cherished, and cared for all those years. I looked at him and said, "It's okay Dad, we will be alright. You did a good job with us, and we know what to do, so it's alright." He just nodded his head and our conversation ended.

Prior to this writing, the only person I ever recall telling this conversation too was my mom. Her response was simple. "Not yet. Your brother is not back yet," she said referring to my oldest brother, Sterling, who was out of state on a church retreat with his family.

Puzzled, I asked, "What does that have to do with anything?"

"Because," she said, "Your Dad will not leave this earth, no matter how much pain he is in, without seeing all his kids."

THE INSPIRATION

True to form and regardless of his pain, my Dad hung on until Sterling and his family came out to the hospital to see him. And not to be outdone, when I went out to the hospital the next day, Dad looked particularly chipper. There was something different about him, but I could not identify what it was.

As I eyed him up and down like Lieutenant Columbo searching for a clue, Dad asked, "What's wrong?"

I replied, "There's something different about you, but I don't know what it is."

Dad raised his arms and I shouted, "They took the IVs out!"

When the nurse came in, I asked, "When did you all take the IVs out?"

The nurse's reply was very sassy, but more than likely she was pissed off. "Ask your father," she said. Dumbfounded, I looked at him and she continued with, "Since he's the one that took them out."

"What do you mean he took them out? I asked. "He can't do that!" I said.

"Well, apparently he didn't get the memo because when we came in for the one o'clock check, the tubes were out with blood everywhere."

Confused, I asked, "What does all of this mean?"

"It means," she said, "That Mr. Randolph is going home, just like he said he was."

The nurse explained that if Dad was stable without the IVs and wanted to go home, they had no choice but to release him. Because the IVs had been out for over eight hours, Dad was going home either later that day, or the next day. All I could do was look at him and shake my head. Dad looked at me like What? What did I do?" I called the house to let Mom know what was going on.

Commissioned as an Army officer in the late 1980's, I was taught officers had two responsibilities: The accomplishment of the mission and welfare of the men, in that order. This experience however, taught me that welfare of the men—and soon after, the women—was first and foremost. Although I had always taken care of the men first anyway, this experience caused me to reflect and ask myself a few key questions:

1. Am I taking care of the job, or taking care of the people?
2. If I take care of the people first, will the mission be accomplished equally well?
3. If I *really* take care of the people, will the mission be accomplished even better?

4. Have I made "the people" My People?

Without "the people," missions are not accomplished. I made 'the people' My People and am very possessive in that area.

My People sort of became my new rallying cry and impacted me throughout my life. Dad was home for my birthday but unfortunately four days later on Monday, October 7, 1991, Burl Wesley Randolph passed in his sleep with my mom, my wife Terry, and me by his side. I was devastated. After things quieted down that morning, I had to call back to Fort Hood and let my crew know what happened. I spoke with Sergeant First Class Richard Phillips, who was my Noncommissioned Officer in Charge (NCOIC). He provided his condolences and said, "Sir, don't worry, Sergeant Ski and I got this. Just be with your family. We will take care of everything else." Sergeant 'Ski' was Staff Sergeant Jerry Koshinski, the Assistant Battalion S2 NCOIC.

The "got this" was in reference to the infamous battalion Nuclear Surety Certification. We had Dad's funeral on Saturday, October 12, 1991, the same day that Redd Foxx had a massive heart attack on the set of The Royal Family, a highly successful sitcom he starred in with Della Reese. Whenever I hear Louis (Louie) Armstrong's song "It's a Wonderful World," I think of both Dad and Redd Foxx. Because my younger sister Debora was born on October 15th, our Mom theorized that Dad had carefully orchestrated his death with God: "Just like your father would not leave without seeing all his children, he would also never spoil your sister or your birthday by his death." I like to think that she was right.

THE APPLICATION

The following series of events provided the lesson for me of what compassion meant. Although we had lost Dad several years earlier, and I saw and experienced what compassion meant, I had not really *learned* the lesson. Much had happened between 1991 and 1999. In that time span Terry and I had moved four times, which included a three-year assignment in Germany. I had switched officer branches (job specialties) from Field Artillery to Military Intelligence. I had successfully completed Company Command (Regional Manager) in Germany. Company Command is a critical position for an Army Captain to successfully execute to be competitive for promotion to Major and serve in junior executive positions in the Army.

Returning to the US from Germany, I served with the Defense Intelligence Agency (DIA) in the Washington, DC, area, where I was promoted to Major. Most importantly, Terry and I began a family. Dominic Marcus Randolph was born, a welcome addition to our family, and we had great joy! That was until I received my next assignment as the Battalion Executive Officer at the Beckley Recruiting Battalion in Beckley, West Virginia. In the almost 10 years we had been married, I had only heard Terry utter a profanity once. Telling her that we were going to West Virginia was the second time. Once the initial shock sank in, we accepted the assignment with trepidation but moved forward anyway.

As the Battalion Executive Officer (XO) (Chief Operating Officer (COO)), I saw my job as enforcing standards, and as anyone can tell you, I was good at my job. I felt that the best approach was a Mr. Spock-like persona from Star Trek: no emotions. I informed the staff that I only had three rules:

1. I'm the boss.
2. I just want the work done.
3. If you have a problem with number two, see number one.

Although this was not the first time I had worked with civilians, it was the first time I had led them and my first time in Army Recruiting. Unaccustomed to any sort of real drama but only Soldier issues, the Spock-like persona was likely not the best approach. The CEO even told me once, "XO, you have to be more compassionate." My response was simple: "No sir, YOU have to be compassionate because you are the commander. My job is to enforce standards." Little did I know that my persona would be crushed like a soda can in five months.

I had two coworkers who were terminally ill. The shocking part is that they were both significantly younger than me. I was young back then with a full head of hair! For their privacy I will only use their first names, but I can tell you something about each of them, because they had similar qualities.

Both women, Kim and Donna, were excellent coworkers that everyone on the staff loved and adored. Both had fought their battles before and placed the enemy, cancer, into remission. Both women had a deep and abiding loyalty to their coworkers, the organization, and their families. Both women reminded me of Dad from the standpoint that neither was ready to leave *their people*. I came to know both well over the ensuing months and years. When Kim died five months after my arrival, we were all devastated.

Because the CEO was traveling to the branch offices, it fell on me to notify the command of the death. I began with my staff because I was the first one notified. They had no idea why I called them together and when I told them of the passing, it was gut-wrenching. I asked if we could hold hands and pray together for strength from God to keep us together, and to help Kim's family during their time of loss. Next, I had to notify the higher headquarters of what occurred using something called a Serious Incident Report (SIR). All deaths were reported directly to the Commanding General (A two-star General). It took what seemed like hours for me to write the notification, pouring over each word.

The ensuing actions and preparations for the funeral were arduous for a Mr. Spock disciple. The amount of raw emotions and compassion I witnessed melted away the facade and required me to interact with my staff in a different manner. Although I understand loyalty, I had to learn how to become compassionate.

The next series of events over 19 months allowed me to display compassion no matter how hard I tried to resist it. As an Iron Major, a term the Army uses for Majors in certain positions, it was difficult to transition from what I had known for the last 10 years as a tactician. As a junior executive my thinking needed to become more operational and sometimes strategic. I was required to transition from focusing on my technical skills to my interpersonal skills. This was a necessary conversion to be successful at the executive level.

I will not recount all the incidents that caused my evolution but focus on how I came to know Donna better. I will mention one event however, and that was another new and welcomed addition to our family: the birth of Derek Michael Randolph! With so much pain around us, our new bundle of joy brought happiness to everyone.

The reason I became Donna's supervisor was because of an administrative glitch with the assignment of Donna's current supervisor, Captain Paul Dwigans. Paul was eligible to depart his current assignment as our Chief Personnel Officer (S1) and Chief

Supply Officer (S4) after two instead of three years. The CEO and I allowed him to leave and we parsed out his duties between the staff sections he oversaw. I temporarily (five months) became Donna's supervisor and had to deal with an unexpected occurrence: the return of her cancer. Because I was her supervisor, Donna felt compelled to tell me everything about her condition, family life, and what she was going through. I believe that I knew as much about Donna's condition as I did my dad's. Two days prior to the departure for my next assignment, Donna died.

Donna did not want tears but joy about her release from pain. Her funeral was the first Celebration of Life event that I had ever attended, and likely still is. I say this because the entire viewing room at the funeral parlor was filled with all the things that Donna liked. Pictures, artifacts, ornaments, anything that made Donna happy was in that room. I believe that is why I never shed a tear or had a sad moment for my coworker and friend, because she also did not want that from anyone.

Being on orders for the new assignment with a specified report date, Terry, Dominic, Derek, and me departed back to the Washington, DC area.

Kim, Donna, and essentially my entire C-level staff illustrated for me the lesson Dad had taught me, but I had not embraced. Compassion is a necessary quality for successful leadership. The CEO, Lieutenant Colonel Thomas McCool, told me that his job was to prepare me to be a CEO. He reinforced the lessons of humility, respect, selflessness, and fearlessness that we all need to be successful in life. It also was the beginning of my knowing how to apply compassion and loyalty on life's journey.

CHAPTER TWENTY
REST AND REFLECTION: RAWHIDE

"*K*now when to rest the horses" Burl Randolph

I often wish I had learned to ride a horse. Do not get me wrong, I have ridden a horse before. I believe that it would be almost impossible to have served as an officer in the famed 1st Cavalry Division and have never ridden a horse. My dilemma is that I do not *know* how to ride a horse. Surviving a short excursion on horseback is not riding or knowing how to ride a horse.

To my knowledge, Dad knew how to ride a horse and was likely an expert as a Cavalryman, but he never shared that experience with us. Dad collected horse statues, spoke to me sometimes in a cavalry language that was foreign to me at the time, and he seemed to regale in his days on the farm and in the service. Although I can "Mount Up," it will not be the same at this stage in my life without my Dad. I learned a great deal however, from his experience as a horse lover.

THE INSIGHT

"Pack em uppppp. Movem out!" For many of us mature readers, this is a signature line from the television show *Rawhide* with Clint Eastwood, known as Rowdy. Unknown to me at the time, it was the cavalry language that I heard from my Dad. During our fishing exploits, that phrase became a sweet surrender on those days that the fish were not biting, I wished I were somewhere else, and my wish was about to come true.

When Dad uttered the command, *pack em up and movem out*, that meant we were going home. The first time I heard him say it, I looked at him like he had lost it. Always curious, I asked where that phrase came from. He said that was the command to move out after the rest period for the horses was over with. "For the horses?" I exclaimed. "Who cares about the horses?" I said.

He looked at me sternly and said, "A good rider always knows when to rest the horses."

I learned much later that the term "rider" could just as easily be replaced with "leader." I would also realize that the horses could be described as the thoroughbreds we all were when we were younger. Consequently, the thoroughbreds are who do the bulk of the work in an organization. Although I heard this phrase at a very young age, I never applied it until long after Dad died.

THE INSPIRATION

The concept of "rest" was not very intuitive to me until much later in my leadership journey, although I saw it modeled throughout my life. Dad was very methodical in what he did, well-reasoned, and understood the need for enough rest. He likely learned this from growing up on a farm and doing strenuous work. This was followed by serving in a segregated military during World War II and the rigors that must have entailed. He then spent the next nearly 30 years tirelessly working to support raising a family. My Dad's role modeling and my experience at the US Army War College are what provided me the true appreciation for rest, relaxation, and reflection.

As we engage in the hustle and bustle of life, attempting to climb the corporate ladder or just make ends meet, rest is vitally important. Although I will outline my thoughts here, The Application will provide the alignment between my Dad, my military experience as a CEO, and my education at the War College. Just as I did, you must answer the following questions for yourself.

1. **Are you getting enough rest?** Regardless of your age and how fit you believe you are; rest is vital for mental acuity and physical stamina. As an Army Captain I could function adequately on four hours of sleep, with

six hours being optimal. As my career progressed and my body aged, this was no longer the case. *Is adequate sleep good enough? What may you be missing from a lack of sleep?*

2. **Do you know how to relax?** I will be the first to admit it: I did not know how to relax. After Dad died, I was so intent on Staying Engaged that I forgot about resting my horses. Relaxation is a stress reliever and is good for the mind, body, and soul. If you subscribe to the theory that "I can relax when I'm dead," you may prove that theory sooner than later. *How do you relax?*

3. **Do you reflect on life?** Reflection is the meditative strategy of self-evaluation. We remember other people's actions, which is an outward activity, but reflection is introspective. I often hear the cliché regarding doing the same thing repeatedly but expecting a different result as insanity. It is more likely a lack of reflection. *Are you confident enough to discover the impact of your actions?*

Rest, relaxation, and reflection are what I referred to at the War College as The Triple R Ranch, my oasis for recuperation. I was selected for the War College after serving 36 months as a Battalion Commander, and while assigned to Fort Bragg, North Carolina, and the XVIII Airborne Corps. My respite was deferred while assigned to the XVIII, serving for 22 months as the Assistant Deputy Chief of Staff for Intelligence. Of my 22 months, 15 were in Iraq. Once again, and I was promoted in Iraq, this time to Colonel. I had not rested, relaxed, or truly reflected for a sum of five years, and it was time.

THE APPLICATION

This may be one of my favorite stories because my decision regarding rest caused me to instantaneously recall Dad. By the time I decided that I needed a rest, I had spent 24 months as a Battalion Executive Officer (XO) (a Chief Operating Officer) and then 36 months as a Deputy and Site Commander in Russia. Part of my Site Commander time was spent training for deployment to Operation Iraqi Freedom (OIF) One. I served as a Senior Intelligence Officer with coalition forces.

I forgot to mention that just prior to deployment for OIF One, I was selected for Lieutenant Colonel and Battalion Command. After returning from Iraq, I was notified that I would assume command of the Baltimore Recruiting Battalion, the largest recruiting battalion in the Army. I ranked this assignment number one on my Command Preference sheet at the time because my mother-in-law was gravely ill, and I wanted us to be closer to her. After being back in the United States for a year, I was still traveling back and forth to Russia. We finally moved to Laurel,

Maryland, which borders Fort Meade, Maryland, where my headquarters was located.

Because I was such a successful recruiting battalion XO, I guess I was rewarded by receiving my first choice of assignments. WRONG!!! My preferences played a very small role in my assignment, but my performance was the main factor. That and probably the fact that no one else wanted the job.

I had a year to prepare and spent it reconnecting with previous noncommissioned officers, tracking the data of the organization, and formulating my game plan. Recruiting was not the tea-and-crumpets assignments I had grown accustomed to. Being at defense agencies in the Washington, DC, beltway had spoiled me, so I was understandably on overdrive.

I remember the phone call from the one-star (Brigadier General) Deputy Commanding General from the United States Army Recruiting Command (USAREC) like it was yesterday. It was a hearty "Congratulations and Welcome." A tutorial on the journey I was about to embark. The conversation was exhilarating, except for the final comment that really got me spinning. "Just remember, your AO [Area of Operations] has the Pentagon in it, with 348 General Officers who are ready, willing, and able to provide you all the advice you never asked for. Welcome aboard." Click.

That clicking sound was the phone hanging up. Everything before the last comment was lost, and I do not recall anything after that comment besides the phone hanging up. I was not in fear or despair, just a bit stunned. Shortly thereafter, the Brigade Commander called me and then the Battalion XO. The Brigade Commander was very direct about hitting the ground running, the need for speed in meeting the mission, and reminded me that the country was still at war. Having just returned, I knew the country was still at war, but now the enemy photographed and televised beheadings of US personnel. This really placed a damper on the recruiting drive.

Within a day or two the Battalion XO called to receive my current contact information: work email address, phone number, and cellphone number. I asked him how the Army Stop Loss had impacted the battalion, and he said that it had not. Stop Loss was when the Army froze all assignments to support a major contingency and, in this case, the war effort. One day during the next week the XO called to inform me that he checked into Stop Loss and 100 recruiters had just been detained with only 20 families volunteering to stay. I replied, "So, what you are really telling me is that I will have 80 pissed off families when I get there?" Unaccustomed to such bluntness, the XO simply said, "Yes, sir."

The next year flew by. I had a kidney stone just four months prior to taking command and arrived at the unit two months early. Once I took command, I began working seven days a week to move the unit in a better direction while recruiting during a time of war. We pushed hard daily to "fill the foxholes" in Iraq, new recruits shipped out as early as seven days after contracting, and we worked on Saturdays with the Military Entrance Processing Station (MEPS) to increase enlistments. This required the organization to work six days a week.

After taking command, I addressed the battalion and polled the audience to determine how many noncommissioned officers and officers had deployed to OIF. Out of 350 Soldiers, only four of us raised our hands. I believe that is what strengthened my resolve to accomplish the mission.

At the 60-day mark, the Brigade Command Sergeant Major (CSM) approached me and my CSM and said, *"Sir, you are pushing the battalion too hard."* I believe my only response was, "CSM, tell that to the commanders deployed in Iraq and Afghanistan."

As I mentioned, I had a plan that involved relentless pressure for 90-days, and then easing up just a bit. At the 90-day mark we were directed to alternate time off for the recruiters with one weekend off per month. My CSM agreed that we needed time off and remarked, "Sir, you gotta know when to rest the horses."

Not having heard that phrase in nearly 15 years, I was transported back to fishing with Dad. I made the decision that there was only one way to give the battalion the time off we needed: to Stand Down. A Stand Down Day is when you take everyone "offline" for a training event, normally for safety, equal opportunity, etc. I decided that this would be for rest, relaxation, and reflection.

The other alternatives were to pick and choose which recruiting stations stayed open on which weekends. Unfortunately, this meant that the battalion and company headquarters would still be required to work every weekend. This was not feasible to the health of the organization, so I made the decision that we would all take off on the first weekend of the month. "Sir, you know that you could get relieved from command for doing this," my CSM advised me. I replied, "But they can only fire me once."

The key was that no recruiting station would be open, no recruiters would work, and no exceptions. This bold move would only work if everyone followed my orders, the CSM and I took the risk, and that our production did not falter. We took our first Stand Down Day.

We returned to work the following Monday, refreshed, renewed, and without incident. If anyone violated my directive, I never found out, and our production increased. I never shared my "strategy" with my peers or anyone else. The Battalion routinely shared the first weekend of the month off, worked two of the three remaining weekends, and steadily improved the unit. Leaders' and Recruiters' attitudes began to improve, our home lives were better, and our battle rhythms became solidified.

I even began taking a quarterly sabbatical to evaluate myself as a leader, husband, father, and person. Not that I required the rest more than anyone else, it was just that with my introverted nature, I needed the means to recoup and get the job done. The importance of rest cannot be understated, even in retirement. A lack of sleep has reportedly been linked to weight gain, stress, and diminished capacity to perform at work. I can relate to this even better in retirement, as my body has adjusted downward from the adrenaline highs of being an Army officer, and I need more rest than I ever thought possible. Adequate rest also improved my creativity.

Resting the horses was a lesson I learned early in life, applied later, and will continue to apply throughout my remaining days.

CHAPTER TWENTY-ONE
CREATIVITY: CORNBREAD, BURL, & ME

Create your own opportunities.

My dad was always making something. He made jellies, jams, preserves, chow-chow, and relishes. He also taught me how sausage is made, literally. Cleaning and preparing fresh fish of all types and wild game, like squirrels, rabbits, etc., and maybe even making candy once or twice a year, especially peanut brittle.

Dad always had a garden and as kids we were *privileged* enough to learn how to shuck corn, hull peas, snap green beans, and pick apples, peaches, okra, and tomatoes. Yes, we lived in the city, but Dad always had a garden in the back yard. When he bought the vacant lot next door, I thought we were like the Jefferson's from television: *Movin on up.* I soon learned that it meant more work for me.

If you recall, the rotary tiller I assembled in Chapter Nine – Figure It Out, that additional land purchase was another garden. Before his heath declined, Dad tended to three gardens in the neighborhood and we (the sons) became well versed in plowing, hoeing, raking, planting, and cultivating. That is likely why I have such a love for plants today.

Dad also made apple cider, peach brandy, and likely several other concoctions I was too young to know about. Food was not something we lacked in the Randolph household. Fortunately, and unfortunately, I never missed a meal. The fortunate part was that we were blessed to always have plenty of food. The unfortunate part was the weight I have struggled with my entire life. Now that I have you thinking about food, there was another item on the menu that made no sense when I heard about it but loved it once I tasted it.

THE INSIGHT

Growing up, cornbread was a staple in our household. We normally had at least two green vegetables at every dinner meal, and cornbread was the starch of choice to accompany that. We had it pan fried, referred to as "skillet cornbread," which looked like pancakes, only much thicker. The favorite cornbread, however, was oven-baked pan cornbread. Although both were made with white corn meal, oven cornbread was more like cake than bread. My four sisters learned how to prepare these various dishes from our mom, but there was one that never seemed to make the cookbook: cracklin' cornbread.

I realize that throughout this book I have not always used the King's English when writing, speaking, or detailing certain items and events, but hey, that just goes to the cultural diversity in America. I had no idea what crackin's or possibly cracklings were back then. To me, they simply looked like small, dried up pork rinds you might normally purchase in a bag from the grocery store. In a sense they were, however, they were not light, fluffy, and easy to chew like pork rinds. They appeared hard, were hard to chew, and I saw no culinary value in them. That was, until I ate them in cornbread.

Once the cracklin's were baked inside the oven-style pan cornbread, they were delectable! The cracklin's made the cornbread moister, more full-bodied, and less like cake and more like bread. The only problem was that you had to eat cracklin cornbread while it was piping hot because once it cooled off, you could break a tooth trying to chew! Of all the things Dad came up with, I had to ask, "How did you come up with this?" His answer was a simple one, "Sometimes you create what you want."

I did not realize that simple answer was the basis for many of the things Dad did. Creativity was not always about necessity, but often about opportunity.

THE INSPIRATION

Cornbread, Burl, and Me is a play on the title of the movie *Cornbread, Earl, and Me*, except my life is not a movie. Out of all the things I watched my Dad create, I found this one the most interesting. Although Mom did the cooking, it was not her idea to add cracklins to cornbread, and it was not something she prepared very often. Maybe only twice a year or three times at the most we had cracklin cornbread, if Mom was feeling generous or we asked nicely.

I have found that people often look to improve something versus create something. When people do create something, their concept is often not concrete in their own minds. I once worked for a Lieutenant General who said,

Guys, I already know what I want to do from start to finish. Most leaders who reach this level do. I can see it in my mind, every detail and how it should work, but I can't do it alone. I need you guys to catch-up and validate with a plan what I already have in my mind.

Some may say that what I just described is vision, what you see in your mind versus with your eyes. That may be true, but I believe that great vision is borne out of great creativity.

For those creative souls reading this, ask yourself a few questions to determine if it truly is creativity or just a good idea:

1. **Has your concept already been done?** As creative as we believe we are, many things have already been created. For example, when you decide to write a book and think you have the best title in the world, think again. A title search may prove you right, but wrong for your book. It is a great title, and it has already been taken. *How will you determine the originality of your creative concept?*

2. **How was your concept borne?** How did your concept come to you? Was it a dream, a blinding flash of the obvious, or brought from frustration? Or did you see something that you thought needed an improvement, and you thought you had the best idea? *How will you approach originality versus extension of a current product?*

3. **How detailed is your thinking about your concept?** Did the Good Idea Fairy visit you and now you are on fire with no idea how to proceed? Concepts cost time, talent, and treasure. Do you have all three in some measure, or will you require significant help? *Can you begin your concept with the end in mind?*

4. **How committed are you to your concept?** Do you have the time, treasure, and talent to bring your concept to fruition? If anyone else is more committed to your concept than you are, maybe it is not really your concept to pursue.

How bad do you want to see your concept become a reality?

5. **What skin-in-the-game are you willing to commit?** I have previously mentioned the Three Ts—time, talent, and treasure. People approach me constantly with their concepts and expect me to bring them to completion. Honestly, I can create just about anything for a price. *What price are you willing to pay for your concept?*

Creativity is not free. However, when creativity occurs, whether through necessity, reality, or originality, there must be enough detail, dedication, and obligation to see the concept through. I had a bright idea in my second CEO position that could have cost me everything if the concept failed.

THE APPLICATION

I chose carefully to share this story, but without trepidation. My creativity was manifested from necessity and reality. It was 2004, and I had just taken over as the CEO of the Baltimore Recruiting Battalion. Baltimore was the largest recruiting battalion in the Army which covered two Metropolitan Statistical Areas (MSA): Washington, DC, and Baltimore, Maryland. Our Area of Operations (AO) was north to south down Interstate 95 and from the Aberdeen Proving Ground Maryland to Norfolk, Virginia. From east to west we touched the shores in Maryland, Virginia, and Washington, DC, over to three counties in West Virginia. For some odd reason the Richmond to Roanoke, Virginia, east to west corridor was not in my jurisdiction, but we had plenty of territory anyway.

The events of 9-11 were still fresh and fighting occurred on two fronts: Afghanistan and Iraq. I took command in June 2004, and by September 2004 Al Qaeda (AQI) was conducting public beheadings of captured American citizens overseas. Naturally the American public was fearful of enlisting into any military branch and recruiting numbers were down. We were working six days a week and our Army Recruiters, the NCOs who sought out civilians for military service, were becoming exhausted. Something had to be done to improve our chances of making our enlistment mission.

The Army is very good about training you for whatever assignment they give you or you volunteer for. CEO or command positions in the Army are extremely competitive, sacred, and voluntary. Once selected and accepted, CEO training, referred to as the Pre-Command Course (PCC), could last at a minimum of four weeks and up to four months for some commands in various stages. I had completed the Army PCC at Fort Leavenworth, Kansas, in February 2004 (a real joy) and the United States Army Recruiting Command (USAREC) course in July 2004 at Fort Knox, Kentucky. The USAREC PCC had two phases: Phase One was instruction, and 90 days later Phase Two was application.

Phase Two reminded me of *Showtime at the Apollo* or *The Gong Show*. Whatever assignment you were given in Phase One you were required to explain in Phase Two, and if necessary, why it should be funded. Lieutenant Colonel John Neal and I were paired to explain Market Expansion. John decided to explain the Employment of Centers of Influence (COI) in Market Expansion and I created Sports Entertainment as a Venue for Market Expansion. From the very beginning this concept was met with resistance because it meant partnering with local colleges, universities, and professional sports teams to recruit at their events. This also involved contracts, legal reviews, strict and continuous oversight, and most of all, *results*.

With approximately six million enlistment-age citizens in my AO, there was no way our Recruiters could reach all of them. I thought, *Why chase the targets when you can just go to where they are?* In our service area, we had at least six major-league sports teams and over 100 collegiate athletic teams. My concept had three objectives:

1. Greater access to our target market.
2. Greater quality in our target market.
3. Greater volume of prospects for our target market.

The structure was divided into two elements: Professional Sports Entertainment (PSE) and College Sports Entertainment CSE).

Our seven regions were heavy with either PSE, CSE, or both. We used a very sophisticated Events Calculation Matrix to determine the output we needed to achieve our required contracts. I cannot take credit for creating that technical tool as I had a genius of a person in Advertising and Public Affairs (APA) Chief, Matt Fullerton. Matt was a retired Master Sergeant (MSG) who knew recruiting like the back of his hand and loved the numbers. My technical contribution was the Events Tracking Matrix, which incorporated everything Matt said needed to get done and determined if we were doing it!

All of this sounded good, looked good, and briefed well ... until I had to present it. I had been allotted $50k to execute an aggressive marketing campaign, and that was how I chose to use the money. My boss gave me latitude to grow as a leader and our big boss never said a word, but their C-level staffs sure did!

I guess I forgot to mention the sixth and seventh requirements for creativity: broad shoulders and thick skin. The moment of truth had arrived because PCC Phase Two was scheduled for December 2004, right before Christmas.

Six of us were scheduled for that course, and John and I were the first in the lineup to brief. As with any executive briefing, a read ahead was required with enough details to be picked apart. John introduced our portion and briefed first. He was thoroughly questioned about his proposal, but because we were both military intelligence officers, we had Red Teamed each other's briefing. Red Team means looking at something through the eyes of the enemy to identify weaknesses in intelligence and/or a plan. John fared quite well, and I felt quite secure until the Commanding General made remarks after my segment was introduced.

"Well, the great Baltimore Recruiting Battalion Commander," he said. "I have been hearing about this Sports Entertainment Market Expansion for months and have never said a word, so I can't wait to hear what you have to say."

Have you ever heard the sound air makes when being released from a balloon? That is exactly how I felt when the air departed my chest with my confidence along with it. I began my briefing in front of the Commanding General (CG), Deputy Commanding General (DCG), Chief of Staff, USAREC Advertising and Public Affairs Chief, and whoever else was in the room. Those nine slides seemed like 900 slides.

The first slide was an attention grabber to show all our recruiting avenues. The second slide, however, was the moneymaker because it was Matt Fullerton's Events Calculation Matrix. This made the CG sit up and take notice. As he previewed the slide with analytical eyes, my confidence began to slowly return. As the remaining board members sent volleys here and there, John Neal had prepared me well. Using a combination of recruiting and tactical terms operationalized from strategic objectives, I made it to the QUESTIONS slide intact. After all inquiries from the board members were completed, the final comments came from the CG.

He began with, "I must admit, when I first heard about your Sports Entertainment concept, I was skeptical. Based on your briefing, however, the concept has detail, substance, and merit."

Suddenly, the tenor of the entire room changed. The other board members engaged the CG with the merits of my concept, how it was being brilliantly executed, and that we were already seeing the returns on investment (ROI). I felt my confidence fully return and no longer felt like such an oddball. That quickly changed when the CG was asked for his final comments and he replied, "Great concept Lieutenant Colonel Randolph. I just hope you survive the GSA [Government Services Administration] audit."

The room went from dead silence to raucous laughter. The CG looked me straight in the eyes and said, "I'm not joking."

I replied, "Yes sir, I know."

I chose to tell this story because it was likely the most risky but creative venture I engaged in as a CEO. It had all the elements I described earlier: necessity, originality, details, commitment, time, talent, and treasure. With only four months of results behind me, I could have had my creativity stifled and shutdown in favor of tried and true methods. However, the country was at war, the enemy was following a prescribed playbook, and we needed something to reach out to our target audience.

Although this concept went viral throughout the command and was being implemented by my peers in every organization, the treasure component became too much to bear. Our contracts with the colleges, universities, and major league teams were negotiated through carefully cultivated relationships. This meant that the treasure we expended had to pass the FAS-R test: Was it feasible, acceptable, sustainable, and what were the risk? Absent those relationships, many organizations could not survive the GSA audits and the concept was scaled back significantly. From cracklin cornbread to command, creativity is a necessity to obtain the unattainable in life. Those creative moments also taught me to embrace life-long learning to stay creative and engaged.

Annual Training Conference Guest Speaker presentation.
L to R: CSM Miguel Ramos, MG Vincent Boles-Guest
Speaker, and me.

Notes Page

LIFE-LONG LEARNING AND MENTORING

This is only my beginning.

Retirement is a funny thing. We all work toward it, long for it, plan around it, and cannot wait for it to occur. Then, when it does occur, it is like a Charlie Brown line from a Peanuts book when he said, "The anticipation far exceeded the actual event."[35]

Yes, I am a Peanuts aficionado. Most people gravitate toward Snoopy, know a Lucy, and relate to Linus, but I always root for Charlie Brown. Just like Popeye, who had a speech impediment, and Underdog, who was a kind and lovable shoeshine boy, Charlie Brown is the ultimate underdog. The allure of Charlie Brown is that <u>he knows</u> he's the underdog but keeps fighting anyway.

Just as Popeye received his strength from spinach and Olive Oyl, and the lovable Shoeshine Boy was really Underdog, crime fighting superhero, Charlie Brown always fought to be everyone's hero. I can relate to Charlie Brown because I am the same way: I fight to be everyone's hero, especially the underdog.

I am keenly aware that the odds were against me right from the start, or at least I felt that way. I had additional tutoring for reading in the first grade and math in the third grade. My fourth-grade teacher almost got me jumped on by a gang, and fifth and sixth grade is when I learned that HUSKY was not a size, nor a compliment. But much like Charlie Brown, I had an outstanding support system. My mom was my tutor and my four older siblings, my defenders. I was husky because we always had plenty to eat, got plenty of sleep, and had luxuries that maybe others did not.

As a life-long learner I do not believe in epilogues or conclusions because we can learn, grow, and thrive until we physically cannot. My parents were both mentally sharp until the day they died, and it was the body, not the mind or the spirit that failed them. I should be so blessed, fortunate, or lucky, whatever your verbal predilection may be. There were things that my dad knew, and role modeled for me, but I had to learn the lessons on my own.

As a parent and outdoorsman, Dad was an excellent delegator. I learned that skill in the military and then grew into it. Dad understood hierarchy and respected and enforced it. Hierarchy illustrates the flipside of my best virtue, patience. I am impatient with hierarchy because I do not want to wait. I want to soar like an eagle to get things done.

Although I know how to "rest the horses," I am still learning how to rest and reflect this horse—myself. As far as humility, I struggle to stay grounded. God, however, keeps me in check by allowing my sometimes stupidity or arrogance to be the instrument of my own failing. Examples include when I forget my age and incur numerous injuries from overdoing it at the gym, leaving me in pain for a month. Or when I forget where I placed the slides for a big presentation! Or my family's personal favorite: when I cannot find my all-encompassing To Do List of things I need to do or need for them to do. Or maybe I just need more mentoring!

RELATIONSHIPS AND MENTORING

I should have joined the Navy because I love ships. I suppose because I did not join the Navy, my fascination with ships was supplanted by leadership, relationships, and mentorship. The two ships that are inextricably connected are relationships and mentorship, which is why mentoring matters. Although the book focuses on leadership, the result was the ultimate mentorship based on the relationship I had with my father.

We define mentoring as *a voluntary developmental relationship where two people share experiences – one with greater experience, once with lesser experience. Based on mutual trust and respect that creates understanding for the mentee.* The

- 247 -

reason this definition is so important is because my research indicated that the relationship is the critical element in mentoring [36]. This definition is a combination of the Army mentoring definition and my research.

Although I used the lessons learned to develop myself as a leader, the mentorship evolved from the relationship. To test my internal theory, I looked at how I learned the lessons:

a. Voluntarily (for the most part)
b. Developmental (in general)
c. Sharing experiences (between my dad and I)
d. To a less experienced person (me)
e. Based on mutual trust and respect (between us)
f. That created understanding (for me)
g. Based on a relationship (father and son)

There were no lessons I learned from my dad that emerged through punishment, coercion, or fear of my dad, but arose normally from my own lack of understanding. My lack of understanding was normally predicated on one of four things:

1. Lack of maturity (child)
2. Lack of experience (teenager)
3. Lack of knowledge (adult)
4. Fear of exploration or failure

The difference between lacking something and fear is that lacking something may create opportunities to explore. Fear normally creates opportunities to ignore. We ignore saying and doing things and acting in particular ways because we are paralyzed by our self-designated inadequacies. We perpetuate our own fears through a lack of knowledge. Mentoring provides the knowledge we lack through creating an understanding of what we seek. This atmosphere alleviates immaturity, creates experiences, increases knowledge, and eliminates—or at least lessens—fear.

INSPIRATION AND RETIREMENT

After five years in retirement I still do not feel retired. My spirit still wants to soar like the eagles I wore on my uniform for so long. I still have the urge to help people by providing a refinement of knowledge as a coach. I still yearn to help create understanding through mentoring relationships. Although I have resisted it for years, the teaching bug is in my blood, albeit at the doctoral level. Having lived in more than 20 locations, I have always been dedicated to helping my community through volunteerism in local organizations, our church, or the schools our children attended. Even though you may retire from a job or profession, retirement does not signal the end of life or giving of yourself.

I am inspired to continually improve myself, the community I live in, my family, friends, or anyone who I meet. There is a caveat to this statement: *If they desire an improved life.* I will unpack this based on what I have learned in retirement:

1. **Average is as average does**. I have discovered that average people will only do average things but want extraordinary results. *Are you average striving for extraordinary, or will good enough do?*

2. **Not everyone is willing to change.** To improve your status in life normally requires change. Change is a bridge too far for some people when being comfortable will do. *Are you comfortable or changeable?*

3. **Success is not Kool-Aid**. The ingredient for success is not like making Kool-Aid. Regardless of how good I *think* I am, there is no "Add Burl Randolph and stir. *Puff.* Instant success." *Are you willing to work for your success?*

4. **The best intentions are not always good enough**. No matter how well intended an initiative may be, it must survive one and two above. Without above average effort and a willingness to change, even the best proposals can fail.

5. **Some people are the Working Retired**. In the Army we called a person who ceased to contribute because either they planned to retire soon or to quit, as ROAD Soldiers—Retired on Active Duty. Some people are the Working Retired: Still working but acting and contributing as if they are retired. *How many Working Retired are in your organization?*

While I have learned many things in five years, those are the most prevalent and what continue to shape my leadership perspective.

I have also validated that leadership is a verb versus a noun. Leader is a noun because that describes a person. Leadership, however, is a verb that describes what the person does. Dad was a leader who exhibited leadership by the actions he took. This is how I developed my values of Action-Oriented, Results-Based, Value-Driven, and Trusted-Agent. As a leader, I never sat on the sidelines and watched others work. I always felt the need to be part of the team by taking part in what the team did, not just taking credit for the accomplishments. I remain *Inspired, Not Retired*, because there is much work to be done in improving our communities, our world, and myself. I will retire when I feel an appropriate amount of my work is done, and I can look back and think to myself, "I have done my best and it is time to rest."

January 2009 at Al Faw Palace, Baghdad, Iraq, after officiating
a Lieutenant Colonel promotion ceremony.

ACKNOWLEDGEMENTS

I first give thanks to God for providing me the skills, intellect, and courage to share my story, and the spirit to help others.

My awareness that I work better in teams has not escaped me. As my good friend Lonnie Johnson mentioned in the Forward, "…we were both two introverts …". It may sometimes be difficult to relate to people as an introvert because you are most comfortable in isolation. This requires having people who accept your quirkiness for what it is: Just the way you are.

I would like to thank my wife Terry for recommending that I dedicate this book to our sons, Dominic and Derek. She had the pleasure of knowing my father, the sometimes pleasure in knowing me, and the joy of mothering our sons. Thank you for having the foresight to remind me that our sons are our legacy, just I am my Dad's legacy.

I thank my sons, Dominic and Derek, for helping keep me 'Dad Straight' and 'Dad Current'. That means they keep me up to date and knowing when to pull back or push forward.

I thank my siblings for sharing our Dad and filling in the gaps I had about some of the lessons. Dad shared many lessons with us all!

Although Mom is with Dad in heaven, I thank her for saving me from myself on many occasions as she and continued to remind me of Dad's advice for over 20 years.

Many thanks to my editor-in-chief, Rev Teresa Ambler, for helping keep me focused throughout this project.

Thank you to Amelia Forczak and the team at Pithy Wordsmithery as the creative geniuses responsible for my out-of-this-world book cover, copyediting, launch page, and email template. Thank you so much!

Although in Chapter One I mentioned the great leaders who were my direct mentors, there are those who also motivated me to do better: General Daniel B. Allyn and Lieutenant Generals Michael Ferriter, Robert Van Antwerp, Jr., and Guy Swan. Also my Battalion Executive Officer, Major Somport Jongwatana.

Finally, I want to thank all the officers, noncommissioned officers, Soldiers, Department of the Army Civilians, contractors, Coalition partners, mentors, mentees, and business partners that I served with throughout my careers. I learned an enormous amount from everyone and want to thank you for helping shape who I am.

AUTHOR'S BIOGRAPHY

Dr. Burl W. Randolph, Jr., DM is a retired US Army Military Intelligence Colonel with nearly 32 years of service. His service included three combat tours in Iraq, Inspector/Monitor duty in Russia enforcing the Strategic Arms Reduction Treaty (START), and tours throughout the United States and Europe. Dr. Burl last served as the Deputy Chief of Staff for Intelligence and Security, Army Sustainment Command, Rock Island Arsenal, IL. After retirement in 2014, Dr. Burl kept inspired by founding and serving as the President and Chief Consultant for MyWingman, LLC, a Business Leadership and Management consulting company in Davenport, Iowa.

Dr. Burl was conferred as a Doctor of Management in Organizational Leadership (DM) from the University of Phoenix, with a doctoral dissertation on Mentoring and African American Army Captain Success: A Case Study. He also earned a Master of Strategic Studies from the US Army War College, and a Master of Business Administration from Troy State University prior to retirement. Dr. Burl has numerous publications in retirement. Mentoring Leaders Across Racial and Gender Lines: Insight from US Army Officers was published in *Global Business and Organizational Excellence* and serves as the condensed, published version of his 300-page dissertation. In Year Three of his doctoral residency, an instructor urged Dr. Burl to publish his Residency final paper as a peer-reviewed article. This resulted in Changing Steps: A Reflexive Journey in Transition published in *The Journal of Global Health Care Systems*. Dr. Burl also ventured into writing, editing, and self-publishing with two books. He is the co-author of the nonfiction work, *Can God Trust You with Trouble*? and editor for *No Disruptions: The Future of Mid-Market Manufacturing*.

Dr. Burl's community work includes serving as a founder and board member in two nonprofit organizations: Foreign Affairs Counsel and the Midwest Manufacturing Business Coalition (MMBC). He has also served as a board member and adviser for Lead(h)er and is a graduate, facilitator, mentor, and Outreach Coordinator for Reboot Combat/Trauma Recovery for the Quad Cities. Dr. Burl also mentors' doctoral students and military officers and edits doctoral dissertations. Dr. Burl is a member of the University of Phoenix Center for Educational Innovation and Technology Research (CEITR) and is a guest lecturer with the University of Alaska Online, Fairbanks, in the Homeland Security Project Management course.

CONNECT WITH THE AUTHOR AT:

burl@mywingmanllc.com

mywingmanllc.com

1-866-242-2260

Inspired, Not Retired

SOURCES

Bass, B. M. (1995). The meaning of leadership. In J. Thomas Wren (Ed.), *Leader's Companion: Insights on leadership through the ages* (pp. 37-38). New York, NY: Free Press.

Davidson, P.R. (1941). *Historical and pictorial review tenth cavalry of the United States Army camp funston - fort riley, Kansas.* Los Angeles, CA: The Army and Navy Publishing Company, Inc.

Drucker, P. F. (1999). Managing oneself. *Harvard Business Review, 77*(2), 64-74.

Drucker, P. F. (2001). *The essential Drucker.* New York, NY: HarperCollins Publishers.

Gatewood, W.D. (2009). John Hanks Alexander (1864-1894). *Encyclopedia of Arkansas.* Retrieved from https://encyclopediaofarkansas.net

Gentleman (2019). In Merriam-Webster's online dictionary. Retrieved from http://www.merriam-webster.com Merriam-Webster

Goleman, D., Boyatzis, R., & McKee, A. (2002). *Primal leadership: Learning to lead with emotional intelligence.* Boston, MA: Harvard Business School Press.

Gonzales-Osler, E. (1989, June). Coping with transition. *Journal of Psychosocial Nursing & Mental Health Services, 27*(6), 32-3. Retrieved from https://www.ncbi.nlm.nih.gov

Harlan, L.R. (1972, 1983). Booker T. Washington. In Raymond W. Smock (Ed)., *The Booker T. Washington Papers, 2 vols, 12* (1972-); (Reprinted from August Meier, *Negro Thought in America*, 1880-1915 (1963)

Harsh (2019). In Merriam-Webster's online dictionary. Retrieved from http://www.merriam-webster.com Merriam-Webster

History.com Editors (2009). *Booker T. Washington*. History. Retrieved from https://www.history.com

History.com Editors (2009). *W.E.B. DuBois*. History. Retrieved from https://www.history.com

king, bb., & jackson, f. (1975). Everybody lies a little. On *Lucille Talks Back* [CD]. Universal City, CA: MCA Records, Inc

Kirkpatrick, S. A., & Locke, E. A. (1995). Leadership: Do traits matter? In J. Thomas Wren (Ed.), *Leader's Companion: Insights on leadership through the ages* (pp. 133-143). New York: Free Press. (Reprinted from *Academy of Management Executive.* 5 (1991), 48-60.)

Kotter, J. P. (1995). What leaders really do. In J. Thomas Wren (Ed.), *Leader's Companion: Insights on leadership through the ages* (pp. 114-123). New York, NY: Free Press

Military (2019). Military history of African Americans. *Wikipedia*. Retrieved from https://en.wikipedia.org

National Archives (2017). *Lt. Henry O. Flipper*. Retrieved from https:// www.archives.gov

National Association for the Advancement of Colored People (NAACP) (2019). *NAACP history: William Edward Burghardt DuBois*. Retrieved from https:// www.naacp.org

National Park Service (2018). *Colonel Charles Young*. Retrieved from https://www.archives.gov

Penn, L. (1997, Summer). Documenting African Americans in the records of military agencies. *Federal Records and*

African American History, *29*(2). Retrieved from
https://www.archives.gov

RAND Research Brief (1985). *Analysis of early military attrition
behavior*. (R-3069-MIL). Retrieved from RAND
Corporation website: https://www.rand.org

Randolph, Jr., B.W. (2018). *Mentoring and African American
Army Captain Success: A Case Study*. (Doctoral
Dissertation). doi: 10.13140/RG.2.2.22343.19363

Randolph, Jr., B.W. (2018 April 5). Teamwork: Does it make the
dream work? [Web log post]. Retrieved from
https://mywingmanllc.com/dr-burls-blog/f/teamwork-
does-it-make-the-dream-work?blogcategory=
Teambuilding

Randolph Jr, B.W., & Nisbett, K. (2019). Mentoring leaders
across race and gender lines: Insight from US Army
officers. *Global Business and Organizational Excellence,
38*(4), 16-25. doi: 10.1002/joe.21931

Randolph, Jr. B.W. (2019, May 20). Perfection: The fake news
about successful leadership [Web log post]. Retrieved from
https://mywingmanllc.com/dr-burls-blog/f/perfection-the-
fake-news-about-successful-leadership?blogcategory=
Leadership+DevelopmentPerfectionism

Roosevelt, T.R. (2003). *Man in the arena. Selected speeches,
letters & essays by Theodore Roosevelt*. John A. Gable
(Ed.) (Fourth ed.), The "Armed Forces Edition." Oyster
Bay, New York: Theodore Roosevelt Association

Rostker, B.D., Klerman, J.A., & Zander-Cotugno, M (2014).
*Recruiting older youths: Insights from a new survey of
army recruits*. (RR247). Retrieved from Rand
Corporation website: https://www.rand.org

Sackett, P., & Mavor, A. (Ed). (2003). Attitudes, aptitudes, and aspirations of American youth: Implications for military recruitment. *The National Academies of Science, Engineering, and Medicine.* Washington, DC: The National Academies Press

Scab (2019) In Merriam-Webster's online dictionary. Retrieved from http:// www.merriam-webster.com Scab, Merriam-Webster

Shultz, C. (1975-1981). *Snoopy: The authorized biography of a great American.* Charles Schulz Biography of Snoopy and the Peanuts Gang. Trivia-Library.com. David Wallechinsky & Irving Wallace. Retrieved from https://www.trivia-library.com

Turner, L.L. (2018). List of things Dr. George Carver invented with peanuts. *Sciencing.* Retrieved from https://sciencing.comGeorge Washington Carver

Tuskegee University (2019). *The legacy of Dr. George Washington Carver.* Retrieved from https://www.tuskegee.edu

NOTES

[1] Kotter, 1995, p. 114

[2] Drucker (2001)

[3] Bass, 1995, p. 38

[4] Kirkpartick & Locke, 1995, p. 143

[5] Ibid

[6] Drucker (1999)

[7] Davidson (1941)

[8] Military (2019)

[9] Penn (1997, Summer)

[10] Randolph (2018)

[11] Scab (2019)

[12] Randolph & Nisbett (2019)

[13] Gonzales-Osler (1989)

[14] Harsh (2019)

[15] Gentleman (2019)

[16] Goleman, Boyatzis, & McKee (2002)

[17] Turner (2018)

[18] Tuskegee University (2019)

[19] king, bb. & jackson, f., 1975, track 2

[20] Randolph & Nisbett (2019)

[21] National Association for the Advancement of Colored People (NAACP) (2019)

[22] History.com Editors (2009)

[23] History.com Editors (2009)

[24] Harlan (1972, 1983)

[25] National Archives (2017)

[26] National Park Service (2018)

[27] Gatewood (2009)

[28] Randolph (2019 May 6)

[29] Knotts (2017)

[30] RAND Research Brief (1985)

[31] Sackett & Mavor (2003)

[32] Rostker, Klerman, & Zander-Cotugno (2014)

[33] Randolph (2018 April 5)

[34] Roosevelt (2003)

[35] Shultz (1975-1981)

[36] Randolph (2018)

Inspired, Not Retired

Made in the USA
Monee, IL
03 January 2020